SIX CHILDREN

SIX CHILDREN
The Spectrum of Child Psychopathology and its Treatment

Ann G. Smolen

KARNAC

First published in 2016 by
Karnac Books Ltd
118 Finchley Road
London NW3 5HT

British Library Cataloguing in Publication Data

A C.I.P. for this book is available from the British Library

ISBN-13: 978-1-78220-282-0

Typeset by Medlar Publishing Solutions Pvt Ltd, India

Printed in Great Britain

www.karnacbooks.com

To
my grandchildren
Chloe, Oren, Alex, and the little one on the way

CONTENTS

PART II: MILDER PSYCHOPATHOLOGY

EPILOGUE

ACKNOWLEDGEMENTS

I wish to thank my colleague, mentor, and friend Salman Akhtar for his encouragement and support. This book would not have come to be without his guidance and inspiration. I also want to express my appreciation and gratitude to my child analytic supervisors; the late Alex Burland, Jennifer Bonovitz, Ruth Fischer, Henri Parens, and Barbara Shapiro, who patiently journeyed with me through hours of clinical material and taught me so well. In addition, friends and colleagues, John Frank and Corrine Masur, were extremely helpful in brainstorming how we can view child analysis in the future. I also wish to express my deepest gratitude and love to my husband and fellow analyst, Edward Hicks, who is my biggest fan and critic, insistent that I share my work with children. Finally, I am deeply appreciative to the six children and their families depicted in this book. I am grateful to them for all they have taught me, but mostly I am honored to have known them and awed by their courage and determination to know themselves.

Portions of Chapter Two and Chapter Four previously appeared in S. Akhtar (Ed.), *Hopelessness: Developmental, Cultural, and Clinical Realms.* London: Karnac, 2015, 3–22.

Chapter Five previously appeared in S. Akhtar (Ed.), *Betrayal: Developmental, Literary, and Clinical Realms.* London: Karnac, 2013, 19–36.
Chapter Six previously appeared in S. Akhtar (Ed.), *Greed: Developmental, Cultural, and Clinical Realms.* London: Karnac, 2015, 3–20.

Ann Smolen,
Philadelphia

ABOUT THE AUTHOR

Ann Smolen, PhD, is a training and supervising analyst in child, adolescent, and adult psychoanalysis at the Psychoanalytic Center of Philadelphia. Dr. Smolen graduated summa cum laude from Bryn Mawr College and received a master's degree in social work from Bryn Mawr College School of Social Work and Social Research. She received her doctorate from the Clinical Social Work Institute in Washington, DC. Her first profession was as a member of the New York City Ballet. Dr. Smolen has won several national awards for her clinical work, which she has presented both nationally and internationally. Dr. Smolen has published several articles including "Boys Only! No Mothers Allowed," published in *The International Journal of Psychoanalysis* (2009) and translated into three languages. Dr. Smolen is the author of *Mothering Without a Home: Representations of Attachments Behaviors in Homeless Mothers and Children* (Aronson, 2013). She maintains a private practice in child, adolescent, and adult psychotherapy and psychoanalysis in Ardmore, Pennsylvania.

INTRODUCTION

Theoretically anchored and historically informed, *Six Children* is a book about the nuances of child psychoanalysis as these unfold in the encounter with different forms of early life anguish. Addressing autistic, homeless, and hopeless children on the one hand and greedy, betrayed, and angry children on the other, the book attempts to integrate developmental deficits, intrapsychic conflicts, and constitutional givens in evolving a deeper understanding of both severe and milder psychopathology. Ample clinical illustrations are provided and technical interventions pertinent to each of these situations are carefully fleshed out. Equal attention is given to holding and interpretation, family intervention and individual focus, and affect management and mentalization.

Child analysis and child psychoanalytic psychotherapy have been in existence almost as long as adult psychoanalysis. Just as there has been a widening scope in adult psychoanalysis, child analysis too has seen a widening scope. Psychoanalysis is no longer restricted as a treatment for the neurotic child. Child analysts treat children who often face difficult obstacles to normal development, including autism, homelessness, and trauma, to name only a few. In addition, as technology has developed, the institution of the "family" has suffered. Parents and children are often glued to their smartphones and iPads, and many have forgotten how to interact with each other on a meaningful level. In addition, our children are over-scheduled, attending after-school activities daily such as music lessons and competitive sports. Our environment has become competitive-based as children are tutored and high expectations are set giving the message that achievement is paramount. As more and more analysts confront these difficult problems that families in the twenty-first century bring to us, new theories and techniques have evolved.

In this volume I have attempted to address the varied difficulties and complications that child analysts confront in this modern world. It is my hope that I have succeeded in demonstrating, using six cases, the various theoretical models and psychoanalytic techniques that child analysts must make use of in order to treat the complex and multiply determined issues that children and their families bring to us looking for guidance and help. In addition, I hope I have shown how psycho-analysis can help families regain what is most important; relationships where parents and children become more reflective and mindful as they begin to understand each other's minds.

CHAPTER ONE

Child analysis—a brief historical review of its development

O ne of the earliest published papers about a child's treatment was *Analysis of a Phobia in a Five-Year-Old Boy* (Freud, 1909b), often referred as *Little Hans*. Little Hans's analysis holds a special place in the history of child psychoanalysis, as it was the first case study of an infantile neurosis; however, the material was not retrieved from a reconstruction of an adult analysis, but rather was a treatment conducted by the father through Sigmund Freud's instructions. Little Hans's castration anxiety (his presenting symptom) and his Oedipus complex were interpreted by Freud through his understanding of his work with adult patients. Because Freud conducted the whole treatment via the father, there was no real elaboration of child analytic technique, thus confusion developed as future child analysts attempted to differentiate child guidance/parent education from child analysis. It was felt, at that time, that a troubled child was helped through his parents. Child analysts did not have a child analytic technique or a well-defined method of treatment. They struggled with differentiating between parental education and parent guidance and what was deemed child analysis. To complicate matters, there was also confusion as to the differences between child psychotherapy and child analysis. For years to come, the case study of Little Hans was the first introduction to child analysis for child psychotherapy candidates (Young-Bruehl, 2007).

Anna Freud stated that the case of Little Hans "pointed toward a general theory of development" (Freud, 1980, p. 278), but did not contribute to child analytic technique. Anna Freud further clarified that her father "looked to Hans's neurosis, his phobia, for confirmation of a hypothesis about how infantile sexuality components are the motive forces of all neurotic symptoms of later life" (Freud, 1980, p. 279). Anna Freud described her father's hypothesis in *The Infantile Neurosis* when she wrote: "… conflict, followed by regression, regressive aims arousing anxiety; anxiety warded off by means of defense; conflict solution via compromise; symptoms" (Freud, 1970, p. 191). Young-Bruehl points out that Anna Freud summarizes in her book *The Ego and Mechanisms of Defense* when she describes what her father had noted. She writes:

> In the case of Little Hans, it was the task of repression to remove the aggressive wishes (stemming from the anal-sadistic phase); it is the task of reaction formation to transform jealousy of siblings into love for them, exhibitionism into modesty, pleasure in soiling into disgust. Displacement from humans (father, mother) to animals (lions, giraffe, horse) is the order of the day, at the same time as attempts are made to divert threatening instinctual dangers from parental home to more distant parts of the external world. Identification with the aggressor determines the role play in which the child takes on the part of the dangerous, biting kicking horse. Projection externalizes his own bad impulses and makes him experience them as coming from his father. Denial in fantasy or in action serves to assuage the narcissistic injury sustained by the realization of the better physical equipment of the father and the child's own inferiority in relation to the bigger, stronger, and perhaps omnipotent and omniscient man. (Freud in Young-Bruehl, 2007, p. 34)

The case of Little Hans was clearly the prototype for understanding conflict, defense, and symptomology in the child, and child analytic technique was based on this theory. However, Melanie Klein did not agree with Anna Freud (more on the *Controversies* later), and rejected the Little Hans prototype. Klein believed that all childhood problems, no matter the symptoms, were the result of trauma. For Klein, the weaning trauma, or paranoid-schizoid position, was what the Oedipus complex and castration anxiety was for Sigmund Freud, the basis for all neurosis and psychosis (Young-Bruehl, 2007).

Child pioneers: the early years

In the early 1900s, Sigmund Freud had serious misgivings that analysis of children was achievable. After Freud published *The Three Essays on the Theory of Sexuality* (1905d), Freud's students were inspired to study and observe children. They "began to observe and record the behavior of their own children, with regard to infantile sexuality; the Oedipus complex, and castration anxiety" (Geissman & Geissman 1998, p. 95). In 1916 Sigmund Freud wrote about his observation of his own grandson as the 18-month old baby threw his wooden spool and retrieved by its rope over and over, working through his separation from his mother. Anna Freud stated: "he was the most observed infant" (Freud in Ginsburg, 2003, p. 265). Sigmund Freud's students observed their children's play, their games, and their overall general activities as a source of data gathering, which served as a foundation for exploring the inner world of the child. Carl Jung observed infants and trained women to treat children analytically. Jung felt that children under the age of eight-years old were not capable of understanding their thought processes and suggested that an indirect method of working with children was more desirable (Geissman & Geissman, 1998). In the 1920s this view began to change. Hermine Hug-Hellmuth is credited as the first to conduct a child analysis. She was the first to offer new ways of working with and thinking about children. In later years, her early initiatives were elaborated upon by other analysts and developed more fully into a child analytic technique and methodology (Holder, 2005). Freud chose Hug-Hellmuth to represent his work in the field of child analysis because she was totally devoted to his theories and would remain faithful to Freud's doctrine. Hug-Hellmuth published numerous papers from 1911–1924, studying the child's earliest memories. Freud held her work in high esteem and recommended that her theories be utilized, even within his own family. Hug-Hellmuth combined psychoanalysis and education in her treatment of children and in addition she believed that the parents should also obtain instruction and edification from the analyst (Geissman & Geissman, 1998).

Freud analyzed Mira Oberholzer in 1912 and several years later (1938) she emigrated to New York City where "she was considered one of the first child analysts" in the United States (Geissman & Geissman, 1998, p. 33). In Germany, Karl Abraham was treating children in analysis as early as 1916. Abraham "saw no theoretical or practical objection to treating children by analysis" (Geissman & Geissman, 1998, p. 36).

In the 1920s when Anna Freud joined the Vienna Psychoanalytical Society, she was not permitted to treat adults because only medical practitioners were allowed to treat adults in psychoanalysis; however, there was no such rule for treating children, so she became a child analyst. In Vienna, Anna Freud, following her father's tutelage, began to devise theory and technique for child analysis. Simultaneously, in Berlin, Melanie Klein under the teachings of Karl Abraham developed her own theories and technique of child analysis. Both Anna Freud and Melanie Klein emigrated to London where each founded her own school of child analysis (Geissman & Geissman, 1998).

Anna Freud

Anna Freud's first profession was as a teacher and she was involved with a group of socialist educators, including Siegfried Bernfeld, Willi Hoffer, and August Aichhorn. These men influenced her early child analytic theoretical formulations, stressing its educative potential (Schmidt, 2008). She originally began her analytic study of children by observing infants and toddlers at the Jackson Nursery in Vienna in 1924 and 1925, and then when she emigrated to London during the war she continued her observations at the Hampstead Nurseries. Because of World War II, it was not unusual for infants to enter the nursery as young as ten days old and remain until the end of the war. Some of the children were lucky enough to remain in contact with their mothers, but many were not as fortunate. These circumstances made it possible for Anna Freud and her followers to "observe the stages of libidinal and aggressive development, the process and the effects of weaning, and the education of the sphincters, the acquisition of language and the various functions of the ego" (Geissman & Geissman, 1998, p. 98). In addition, the different forms of separation anxiety were noticed for the first time. In 1945, at the end of the war, the Hampstead Nurseries closed, but evolved to become the Hampstead Clinic (and later the Anna Freud Centre) where Anna Freud continued her work and went on to develop the Hampstead Index, which aided her in creating her developmental lines, described in her book, *Normality and Pathology in Childhood* (1965).

Melanie Klein

Like Anna Freud, Melanie Klein was also a lay analyst. Just as Anna Freud was not allowed to treat adults because she was not a medical doctor, the same held true for Klein. Like Anna, she too became a child analyst. Unlike Sigmund Freud who studied the inner life of the child through his conversations with Little Hans's father, and from reconstructions of his adult patient's analytic material, Klein studied childhood conflicts and built her theories by directly working with the child (Geissman & Geissman, 1998). Abraham suggested that she become a child analyst. Klein began to see children in analytic treatment in 1921 and by the time she emigrated to London in 1926 she had already developed her analytic technique using play, which she felt was the child's way of free associating and the ideal method of gaining access to the child's unconscious (Holder, 2005). She felt that the child's internal world is made up of "primitive imagoes, which must be differentiated from the images of reality, modified as they have been by the process of introjection" (Geissman & Geissman, 1998, p. 120). For Klein, the child's mind is bursting with beasts and fiends. Where Anna Freud rejected the death instinct concept, Klein based her theories on it as she "describes an infant whose first movement is not a gesture of pure love towards its object, but a sadistic movement lined to the deflection of the death instinct" (Geissman & Geissman, 1998, p. 121).

The controversies (1924–1944)

Both Anna Freud and Klein presented their concepts and theories about child analysis as early as 1924. Klein presented her technique of child analysis at the Salzburg Conference, while Anna Freud was compiling data and building theory in Vienna where she presented lectures on child psychoanalysis (Freud, 1927), which became an ongoing seminar where child cases were presented and discussed. The child analysts who participated in these seminars were Berta Bornstein, Edith Sterba, Jenny Waelder-Hall, Erik Erikson, Anny Katan, Marianne Kris, Margaret Mahler, and Elisabeth Geleerd (Holder, 2005). When both women ended up in London during the war, the infamous *Controversies* began and a serious divide within the analytic community occurred. While these particular controversies officially ended in 1944 the child analytic community to this day still experiences the repercussions of this bitter disagreement. It is instructive to explore the differences that caused the split within the analytic community.

Anna Freud and Klein disagreed along several major theoretical and technical lines. As stated earlier in this chapter, Anna Freud discarded the death instinct concept, leaning toward Hartman's theory of aggression as a reaction to frustration, while Klein remained steadfast to Sigmund Freud's early conceptualization of the death instinct. Klein understood the death instinct as a clinical theory "regarding it as the main reason for anxieties in infants, who were afraid of destroying themselves and their objects" (Holder, 2005, p. 43). Another dispute was, while Anna Freud was interested in very young children and observed their behaviors, she believed that very young children were not analyzable, stressing that the ability to verbalize was necessary for secondary process thinking (Freud, 1965), which in turn made analysis possible. Klein did not rely on verbal abilities and analyzed very young children using play as a way of accessing the child's unconscious. She demonstrated this by conducting an analysis and documenting it on her own five-year-old son. This important dissimilarity was thought to be the crux of the conflict between the two women, as Anna Freud held steadfast to the idea the "child analysis could only consist in the application of adult analysis" (Geissman & Geissman, 1998, p. 122).

Another important theoretical difference was their divergent conception of the infantile neurosis and how it came about. Anna Freud stated that the infantile neurosis was stimulated by the resolution of the Oedipus complex and castration anxiety. Klein, on the other hand, felt that it developed in the first year of life as a defense against psychotic anxiety. Stemming from these beliefs, Anna Freud thought that only neurotic children were suitable for an analytic treatment, while Klein's work "opened the way for analysis of psychotics, who until then, had been considered to be irremediable because they were incapable of communicating in symbolic terms" (Geissman & Geissman, 1998, p. 126). Anna Freud demonstrated her technique in the case of nine-year-old Peter who lay on her couch and described his dreams, not unlike an adult. This case was conducted through words. Anna Freud stated: "we can apply unchanged to children what we have learned from our work with adults" (Freud, 1927, p. 24). She relied on interpretation and the acquisition of insight to ultimately bring repressed memories to consciousness. It was not until the 1950s that Anna Freud incorporated play materials into her technique. She explored the child's unconscious but connected what was happening in the child's environment to their unconscious conflicts. Anna Freud demonstrates in the case of Peter that she was "sensitive to the very real ongoing impact of the external world ... and took steps to limit the damage being inflicted" (Midgley, 2012, p. 62). Anna Freud also felt that a full transference neurosis was not possible in child analysis because of the child's ongoing dependent relationship with their parents. One of the most controversial concepts Anna Freud put forth was the idea that the analyst must, at times, serve as an auxiliary ego for the child (Midgley, 2012).

Klein, on the other hand focused completely on the child's unconscious and with no interest in the child's real objects, only his internalized objects were of interest to her. She felt, contrary to Anna Freud's theory, that very young children were capable of developing a full transference neurosis. She described her analysis of Dick, a very young child who was probably autistic. She conducted this treatment well before Kanner (Kanner, 1943) described autism (Holder, 2005).

Another critical difference was Anna Freud remained loyal to her father's theory that the superego developed as a direct result of the resolution of the Oedipus complex around age six, while Klein believed that the Oedipus complex was triggered by the weaning trauma, "so that it began under the predominance of hate. Klein later modified this view; although she placed the beginning of the Oedipus complex in the second oral phase, she now associated it with the depressive position and hence with a conflict between love and hate." (Holder, 2005, p. 39)

The two women also devised different analytic techniques in their work with children. Anna Freud stayed true to Hag-Hellmuth's vision that parental education is a vital component of child analytic work. In the early years, Anna Freud made use of a period of time at the beginning of treatment where she attempted to form a positive transference by feeding the child and gratifying other needs. As stated earlier, Anna Freud focused on the infantile neurosis. Melanie Klein did not work with the parents; she used play therapy and saw very young children with a focus on the earliest phases of development (Holder, 2005).

Lastly, Anna Freud and Klein had differing views of the role of the superego and its role in the analysis of a child. "For Klein, the great strength and severity of the early superego was the basis of childhood neuroses, and control of this punitive superego-that is, mitigation of its severity-was the aim of child analysis. Conversely, Anna Freud regarded a child's superego as weak and immature and the child as still too dependent on his parents for a complete analysis of the parent-child relationship to be possible." (Holder, 2005, p. 81)

To summarize: Anna Freud and her followers remained loyal to Sigmund Freud's early theories, while Klein and those who followed her, made use of his later theoretical leanings. The *Controversies* officially ended in May of 1944 and in June 1946 the British Psychoanalytic Society officially named three distinct schools: the Kleinian school where young children were analyzed through the mechanism of play and psychotic children were treated by analysis; the Anna Freud group who studied normal childhood development and the complications that arise within normal development, focusing on neurotic children; and the Middle Group or Independents, led by Winnicott who felt badly that he and his followers were not accepted by either Freud or Klein (Geissman & Geissman, 1998).

Donald Winnicott: Middle Group or Independents

Winnicott trained as a pediatrician and was interested in infancy and the earliest infant/mother relationship. Anna Freud thought of him as leaning toward Kleinian theory and technique and turned her back to him, but the Kleinian group also rejected him. These rebuffs caused him much sadness and resentment, but he went on to be a major force in the Middle Group, also known as the Independents, who were opposed "to any extremist or totalitarian thinking" (Geissman & Geissman, 1998, p. 235). Winnicott placed significance on the influence of the external environment, "which he described as being an ally of the child's ego in the maturational process" (Geissman & Geissman, 1998, p. 221). Winnicott was the first analyst to state that the ruptures between infant and primary caretaker are not of importance but rather it is the repair of such disruptions that are of importance. He focused on these ruptures as impingements to *going on being*, that if not repaired could lead to annihilation anxiety.

Independent of Margaret Mahler's work on separation/individuation in the United States at around the same time, Winnicott wrote about the earliest mother/infant relationship, connecting maternal preoccupation with her infant to separation and independence. Winnicott spoke about the ability of the child to play alone in the presence of the mother and he defined "areas as being inner and outer, internal reality and external reality, transitional area, and cultural areas" (Geissman & Geissman,

1998, p. 220). Winnicott connected his theories of mother and infant to the relationship between the analyst and his patient and the importance of regression and dependency within the transference.

Winnicott contributed to the child analytic literature by developing several important concepts such as *there is no such thing as a infant; primary maternal preoccupation, the good-enough mother, going on being; holding function; transitional space;* and the *transitional object* to name just a few.

Primary maternal preoccupation (1956) is a state of mind of the mother where she becomes inwardly focused toward the end of pregnancy and remains in a state of heightened sensitivity during the first few months following the birth of her infant. Winnicott understood this as a normal state of mind that enables the mother to be attuned to her infant's needs. The *holding function* of the mother stems from her state of primary maternal preoccupation where she identifies with her infant and experiences empathy. In Winnicott's theory, "holding" by the mother is crucial for proper development where the infant goes from "absolute dependence to relative dependence and then to independence" (Geissman & Geissman, 1998, p. 227). Within the holding function, the infant experiences a consistency and predictability as caring for the infant becomes routine and dependable (Wolman, 1991). Holding "is more akin to the function of a jar that holds water" (Wolman, 1991, p. 38). The mother keeps out impingements so that the infant may experience a "continuity of being". *Going on being* (1956) is a phase of development when the infant experiences instinctive psychic development and is "characterized by four elements: spontaneity, authenticity, agency, and continuity" (Akhtar, 2009, p. 123). The state of "going on being" is dependent on the mother's maternal preoccupation and her ability to provide a holding environment. The *good-enough mother* is emotionally available, predictable, and dependable as well as physically present (Winnicott, 1962). This mother "holds the infant not just in her arms but also in her sight and with her voice and in her mind" (Wolman, 1991, p. 41). Winnicott explains *transitional objects* (1953) as a developmental milestone where the infant (from five to twelve months old) is able to make use of an object such as a blanket or teddy bear in the mother's absence. Winnicott's concept of the *transitional space* is directly related to his idea that there is "an area of the mind where reality and unreality coexist ... [this] is where imagination is born and paradox reigns supreme" (Akhtar, 2009, p. 293). It is within this transitional space where creativity flourishes. For Winnicott and his followers, much of the work of analysis lives in the transitional space co-created by the analyst and patient. One of Winnicott's most valuable concepts relates to the rapprochement phase of separation as well as the anal phase of psychosexual development where he "defines the mother's task as learning how to survive her child's attacks. She survives by maintaining her consistency and by not retaliating against her child's aggressive behavior" (Wolman, 1991, p. 41). Winnicott was a pioneer in treating psychotic children and determining that problems during separation-individuation are the origins of borderline and narcissistic psychopathology in adults (Wolman, 1991).

After 1946

At the Hampstead Clinic, Anna Freud concentrated on treatment, prevention, research, and teaching. Anna Freud and Dorothy Burlingham worked together, determining the emotional damage the children endured during the war when separated from their mothers. This gave them the opportunity to determine and prevent disorders that might develop from preventable separations from the primary caretaker and to gain an understanding of separation anxiety. One of Anna Freud's major contributions to child analysis was her concept of development lines. She stressed that the ability to obtain a certain level on any one of the developmental lines is "the result of an interaction between the development of the drives, the ego/superego system, and their reaction to the influence of the child's environment" (Geissman & Geissman, 1998, p. 197).

Another major contribution by Anna Freud was her *Diagnostic Profiles* for psychoanalytic assessment. In collaboration with her colleagues from the Hampstead Clinic, she created profiles for infants, children, adolescents, and adults. From their work on adolescents the European Association for Adolescent Psychoanalysis (EAAP) was established in the 1990s, spearheaded by Moses and Egle Laufer (Young-Bruehl, 2007). Anna Freud was concerned about the field of adolescent psychoanalysis and stated: "adolescence is a neglected period, a stepchild where analytic thinking is concerned" (Freud, 1936, p. 136). Over the next several decades analysts such as Erikson, Blos, and Laufer made major contributions to the understanding this phase of development (Young-Bruehl, 2007), however, Anna Freud held on to her belief that psychoanalysis proper was an appropriate treatment for neurotic disorders and not for more serious cases.

During these years after the war most adult analysts did not recognize child analysis as a viable treatment and thought of it as an inferior profession. Early on both Klein and Freud held the view that adult analytic training should be a prerequisite for child analytic training. However after Anna Freud established the Hampstead Clinic she allowed clinicians to train as child analysts with no prior adult training or experience. Child training at the Hampstead Clinic was available to social workers, teachers, nurses, as well as other lay professionals. The Hampstead Clinic was the first and only training facility that was exclusively dedicated to training child analysts as well as conducting research and offering psychoanalytic treatment to children and adolescents (Holder, 2005). The treatment of children was conducted in three locations in London: the Tavistock Clinic, which was Kleinian; the Hampstead Clinic (later became the Anna Freud Centre), which was Freudian, and Paddington Green Hospital, which was Winnicottian (Geissman & Geissman, 1998).

It was not until the 1950s and 1960s that child analysis became established. The child analysts who had settled in the United States were all from the Anna Freud side of the controversies. They were Peter Blos, Erik Erikson, Heinz Hartmann, Kurt and Ruth Eissler, Ernst and Marianne Kris, Anny Katan, Jenny Waelder, Therese Benedek, Berta Bornstein, Peter Neubauer, and Erna Furman. Melanie Klein and her group were ignored (Holder, 2005). Anna Freud had to fight for her child trainees to be recognized by the International Psychoanalytic Association (IPA). She cited examples of child training centers in Leyden and Amsterdam in the Netherlands and in the United States, the Association for Child Psychoanalysis in New York run by Marianne Kris, and a child center in Cleveland run by Anny Katan and Erna Furman, all of whom were trained in London at the Hampstead Clinic. Even as recent as 1960, the IPA accepted child trainees who were trained by the British Psychoanalytic Society but not those trained at the Hampstead Clinic (Geissman & Geissman, 1998). Only those trained by the British Psychoanalytic Society had the right to call themselves "child analysts" while individuals trained at the other child centers were deemed "non-analytic". Many adult analysts were nasty, displaying their hostility toward child analysts by making comments such as: "When are you going to stop playing with kids and be one of the big boys?" (Schmidt, 2008, p. 50). This statement seems to convey resistance to analytic treatment of children. Those trained at the Hampstead Clinic had the title of "Child psychotherapists" (Holder, 2005). In the United States, it was not until 1958 that the Board of Professional Standards of the American Psychoanalytic Association issued standards for the training of child analysts (Schmidt, 2008).

It is important to note that in 1945 Anna Freud became a co-founder of *The Psychoanalytic Study of the Child*. This illustrious journal formed an editorial team from both the United States (Otto Fenichel, Phyllis Greenacre, Heinz Hartmann, Edith Jackson, Ernst Kris, Lawrence Kubie, Bertram Lewis, Marian Putnam, and Rene Spitz), and Great Britain (Anna Freud, Willi Hoffer, and Edward Glover).

The United States post-war

In 1958, Anny Katan began the Cleveland Center for research in Child Development and in 1964 opened a child analytic clinic modeled on the Hampstead Clinic. Later, with Erna Furman, together they founded the Hanna Perkins Therapeutic School. The Cleveland Clinic offered psychoanalytic treatment to children and adolescents regardless of economic or social class. Their focus of study was in the following areas: mourning, learning disabilities, emotional trauma, adoption, somatic disorders, foster care, child abuse, as well as concepts such as fantasy versus reality and the latency phase of development. In 1965, Marianne Kris and Berta Bornstein founded the American Child Psychoanalysis Association in New York where child analysts were trained. Around the same time, Peter Neubauer founded the New York Child Development Center and the Yale Study Center (Geissman & Geissman, 1998; Holder, 2005).

There were several other prominent analysts who emigrated to the United States and who had significant influence on the evolution of child analysis. Heinz Hartman was a loyal follower of Anna Freud. He developed his theory of ego psychology as a result of his observations of children in analysis at the Hampstead Clinic. Both Anna Freud and Hartman influenced Erik Erikson's work. Erikson established the concept of identity and ego strength. In addition he worked with Gregory Bateson and Margaret Mead who were renowned anthropologists and influenced his understanding of how culture and society impacted human development (Geissman & Geissman, 1998). Phyllis Greenacre viewed birth as the basis of all anxiety and Bruno Bettelheim was the first to unmask the myth of the rejecting mother who was blamed for causing autism in her child. Bettelheim claimed "all mothers, and not just mothers of autistic children, have destructive intentions which run parallel to their loving intentions, as do all fathers" (Geissman & Geissman, 1998, p. 268).

Infant researchers and their contributions to the field of child analysis

In the last sixty years there have been vast changes in our understanding of child development and parent-child relationships. The following infant researchers made major contributions to child analytic theoretical changes based on an interactional point of view. These researchers focused on the dyadic relationship rather then the drive-conflict model. This paradigm change contributed to major changes in child analytic technique. The earliest empirically based mother-infant research is credited to Rene Spitz.

Rene Spitz

One of the earliest pioneers in infant observation/research was Rene Spitz. He undertook a training analysis with Sigmund Freud in 1910. He was one of the few researchers of his time who worked predominantly with direct observations of infants and young children. His most famous and prestigious studies were on severe early deprivation of mothering, which often resulted in "hospitalism", "anaclitic depression", or "auto-erotism" (Emde, 1981). Spitz's first interest was in studying the smiling response in infants. His observations led him to state that the social smile in the infant gave the "impression of striving for, and of pleasure in reciprocity" (Spitz, 1965, p. 99). He was the first researcher to speak of affective discrimination as the earliest mental activity that then set the trajectory for further development.

Spitz wished to understand "the psychological meaning inherent in the child's emotional relations with his human partners" (Spitz, 1983, p. 123), as he described the consequences of maternal deprivation and maternal overprotection. He contemplated the critical impact of the environment and the mother's psychology on development. Spitz was the first theorist and researcher to look at the "mutual exchanges in a give and take action and reaction between two partners which requires from each of them both active and passive responses" (Spitz, 1983, p. 178). Spitz was the first to acknowledge and stress the importance of the interactions between the mother and infant as he described the circular process of these interactions. Spitz stated: "… the child's initiatives provoke reverberations in the mother … which in turn evoke an answering behavior in the child and so on, producing ever new constellations of increasing complexity, with varied energy displacements" (Spitz, 1965, pp. 183–184). From this data he discussed the implications on brain development, the development of the self, and the development of language (Emde, 1981).

One of Spitz's most important contributions to child psychoanalysis and to society was his work with institutionalized infants, coining the term "hospitalism" (Spitz, 1965). Spitz studied children from two institutions. In the first, the children were in a foundling home, in the second group the infants were institutionalized because their mothers were in prison. In this first institution, only the children's physical needs were attended to. He showed a huge contrast in the development of the children based on maternal deprivation. Spitz discovered that children who were institutionalized from infancy developed significant psychopathology and stated that "there is a point under which the mother-child relations cannot be restricted during the first year without inflicting irreparable damage" (Spitz, 1945, p. 70). He set out to determine the "pathological factors responsible for the favorable or unfavorable outcome of infantile development" (Spitz, 1945, p. 56). He determined, following children in the foundling home, that in spite of good physical care such as hygiene and feeding, the children showed "from the third month on, extreme susceptibility to infection and illness of any kind" (Spitz, 1945, p. 58). He made the claim that the presence of a mother or primary caretaker compensated for all other environmental deprivations stating "they suffered because their perceptual world is emptied of human partners" (Spitz, 1945, p. 68).

Spitz hoped that his study of institutionalized infants and children would offer answers for how to help orphaned infants. He also felt that his work had social implications as women were entering the workforce because of World War II.

Two years after his first study comparing institutionalized infants from two different institutions, Spitz did a follow-up study and found that out of the original ninety-one children in his study, twenty-seven had died by the end of the first year. At the end of the second year another seven children had died with total mortality rate of thirty-seven percent. The remaining twenty-one children were found to show extreme retardation in development in comparison to their peers raised by a primary caretaker. In this follow-up study Spitz was concerned that "damage inflicted on the infants by their being deprived of maternal care, maternal stimulation, and maternal love, as well as by their being completely isolated is irreparable" (Spitz, 1946, p. 114). He was unsure if these children would benefit from therapeutic interventions.

Spitz built his theory on the idea that in the beginning there are no objects. He considered the psyche to be unstructured. Like Freud, he felt that the infant reacted to the object purely through physical needs. He divided development into stages stating that in the first stage "emotional organization varies from excitation to quiescence, in the second stage the manifestations of unpleasure and pleasure become unmistakable" (Spitz, 1950, p. 67). However he was the first theorist and researcher to claim that during the first year of life a "twoness rules the development of every new behavior and activity" (Spitz, 1950, p. 68), demonstrating that by the eighth month the libidinal object has been established.

Spitz's groundbreaking research demonstrated that there is a vital relationship between the nature of the environment and the etiology of pathology. He claimed that poor environmental conditions made it almost impossible for a shift from "narcissistic cathexis into neutralized libido" (Spitz, 1950, p. 70), which in turn makes the formation of healthy object relations impossible. Spitz's work was a great contribution to preventive psychiatry and to providing new ideas in how to work therapeutically with children who experience gross early deprivation.

The term anaclitic depression was first formulated by Spitz (1946). Infants after six months of age who experienced prolonged separations from their primary caretaker developed an anaclitic depression. Spitz observed that these infants develop symptoms of weeping, apathy, inactivity, withdrawal, sleep problems, weight loss, and developmental regressions. In addition, feelings of loneliness, helplessness, and fear of abandonment are now understood to be a part of this syndrome. If adequate mothering is re-established within a reasonable time period, the infant is expected to recover. Spitz also described this as an "emotional deficiency disease" (Spitz, 1965); the occurrence of an anaclitic depression was linked by Spitz to the "developmental milestone of the mother's becoming a consistent and recognized object for the infant" (Wagonfeld & Emde, 1982, p. 66). Anaclitic means leaning upon. The infant becomes depressed, as the mother is experienced as not available to lean upon.

Spitz (1965) stated that the manifestations of aggression, normally demonstrated in the infant in the second half of the first year of life, such as biting and hitting are absent in anaclitic depression. He postulated that the aggressive drive was turned back onto the self. Many of these infants develop self-injurious behaviors such as head banging and tearing their own hair. Thus the expression of both libidinal attachment and aggression are inhibited.

Anaclitic depression is related to the establishment of an object tie. Spitz emphasized that the children who develop anaclitic depressions are those who had once developed satisfactory object ties. A good object attachment must first be established in order for its loss to be mourned. Erikson (1950) spoke of the loss of maternal love as a cause of anaclitic depression, which he described as a "chronic state of mourning". He further speculated that infants and young children who suffer from the loss of the libidinal object during the second half of the first year might experience a depressive undercurrent for life.

Margaret Mahler

Margret Mahler made use of Spitz's work, which highlighted the tremendous trauma that could occur with certain types of separation from the primary caretaker. We know that in Spitz's research the infants were physically separated from their mothers for long periods of time. These separations were obviously out of the control of the infant. Mahler saw this as the child being passive in relation to the separation. Mahler's work on separation took a different turn. She looked at the normal process of separation-individuation. In other words Mahler was interested in "the child's achievement of separate functioning in the presence of the mother while the child is continually confronted with *minimal* threats of object loss" (Pine & Furer, 1963, p. 325). Mahler pointed out that normal separation-individuation is a developmental task of all humans. She further stated that the child attains pleasure in his newfound independent functioning because the mother remains libidinally available (Mahler, 1963).

In the classic book *The Psychological Birth of the Infant: Separation-Individuation* (Mahler, 1975), the concept of separation-individuation phases and process are outlined and extensively defined and described. Mahler's work with very young, severely mentally ill children first led her to describe a "symbiotic psychosis" of early infancy (Mahler, 1952, 1968).

Mahler took Spitz's work further and reported that the children she saw had demonstrated normal development to the point when they became separated from their mother. A "rupture [occurred] before he or she was emotionally ready for it, and (in predisposed children) panic, regression, and fragmentation were the result. Stark, panic-driven and overwhelming clinging behaviors (linked to the symbiosis) were often seen, but *secondary* withdrawal into noncontact (autism) was also seen and understood as protective shield against the panic of loss of merger fantasy." (Pine, 1992, p. 104)

Mahler made use of systematic observational research. She studied normal, middle-class children. She observed how they "negotiated the task that the symbiotic psychotic child presumably failed at-that is, the move from symbiosis to self-other differentiation and object relationship" (Pine, 1992, p. 104). Mahler et al. demonstrated in their extensive observational research of mothers and their children, the process of the separation-individuation phase that took place from five months to thirty-six months of age. Mahler divided the separation-individuation phase into four sub-phases: "differentiation, practicing, rapprochement, and the move toward object constancy" (Pine, 1992, p. 104).

Mahler's incredible research produced new theory (separation-individuation theory) and had vital importance to clinical technique as therapists came to understand and make use of her theory. In past years Mahler's work has been criticized based on newer infant research which demonstrates that infants are born with "a degree of perceptual and cognitive sophistication too substantial for the infant ever to have been in a phase where he or she failed to differentiate between self and mother" (Pine, 1972, p. 103). Stern states that symbiosis is only a fantasy that emerges later in life and that the infant is born with an awareness of self and other (Stern, 1985). It is important to note that Mahler "initially intended symbiosis as a metaphor for the child's imagined fusion with the mother" (Wolman, 1991, p. 38).

Selma Fraiberg

Fraiberg was a pioneer in her efforts to help the underserved population who were at high-risk for abuse. In her paper "Ghosts in the Nursery" (1975), she and her colleagues used psychoanalytic concepts to both understand and help young mothers who had been identified as rejecting toward their infants. They understood the mother's unhappiness and saw that the mother's troubled history needed to be addressed in order for her to not pass on, unconsciously, past abuse and rejection to her own infant. What was perhaps most striking is that this work was not done in ones office or clinic but in the kitchens of then young families. This was the beginning of bringing psychoanalytically informed therapy off of the couch, out of the office and to the young families who needed it most.

Henri Parens

Henri Parens conducted his mother-child observational research from 1970 to 1977. He published a nineteen-year follow-up study and thirty-seven-year follow-up study. He saw mothers and children from the Philadelphia Projects twice a week in a mother-child group. Parens began his research with the following idea: he was determined to correlate three separate ego functions with mother/child interactions. Parens initially followed Spitz and Mahler with the intention of adhering to an observational frame. However psychiatric fellows and residents attended some of the sessions and he would point out developmental issues to them. The mothers overheard (as he intentionally did not lower his voice thinking that rude) and asked to be included in the discussions. Thus his strict observational frame, only answering questions when asked, evolved into teaching the mothers about their children's development. Like Mahler and Spitz before him he taped all of the sessions with a hand-held movie camera.

Parens began to notice what he determined was neutralized aggression in babies as young as 15 weeks. All theory to this point stated that the ego of such a young infant was not mature enough to neutralize aggression. He commented: "The babies had not read Freud!" (Parens, 2006, personal communication). He began to ponder Freud's theory on aggression stating that he threw out the old model and focused on the behavior of the infants he was observing. This struggle took many months and culminated in a dream. When he woke he had discovered a new model of aggression (Parens, 2006, personal communication). Parens came up with four categories of aggression all postulated on the position that hostile aggression is generated by extreme pain (Parens, 1979). These are: "(1) the unpleasure-related discharges of destructiveness, (2) the nonaffective discharge of destructiveness, (3) the nondestructive discharge of aggression, and (4) the pleasure-related discharge of aggression" (Parens, 1979, p. 4). Thus his research looking at correlations of ego functions and mother-child interactions was derailed and in its stead he formulated a totally new theory of aggression. In addition he was the first researcher to incorporate parent education with mother-child observation. From this research, Parens also developed a new path of Oedipal development for the little girl (Parens, 1976).

Parens' research began with mother-infant observation and evolved into a program for parent education. From this extensive research Parens developed a new theory of aggression and suggested a different path by which the little girl enters the Oedipal complex. His findings add to and change technique as the analyst might think differently about aggressive behaviors and understand the little girl's Oedipal phase of development in a new way.

Stanley Greenspan

Perhaps the most important contribution from Greenspan has been his longitudinal research study with NIMH where he explored the parent-infant relationships defining multiple variables. His work involved helping mother/infant dyads who were at high risk for attachment difficulties. Greenspan developed a team approach where many services were put in place for these high-risk families. In addition to studying the parent-infant dyad, Greenspan was dedicated to determining intervention techniques. Greenspan developed a theoretical structure which he termed "the developmental structuralist" approach. Greenspan based his theory on two assumptions:

> that the child's organizational capacity changes over time to higher levels, so that stimuli (internal and external) of increasing complexity are processed in such a way as to lead to the development of structures of parallel complexity; and that each succeeding stage of development epigenetically builds on the resolution of the characteristic tasks of the preceding stage. (Shopper, 1984, p. 122)

Greenspan (1981) describes the following five stages:

1. Somatic level of organization, phase I, homeostasis (birth to three months)
2. Phase II attachment (two to seven months)

3. Phase III somatic-psychological differentiation (three to ten months)
4. Phase II behavioral organization, initiative, and internalization (nine to twenty-four months)
5. Representational capacity, phase I, representational differentiation, and consolidation (thirty to forty-eight months)

Greenspan states that at each stage an adaptive structure must form in order to move ahead to the next stage. Most interesting in this work is that once disordered development has been identified a preventive intervention is designed for the individual parent-child dyad (Greenspan, 1981).

Like Parens, Greenspan worked with an underserved population who presented with multiple problems. These families required a special support staff and outside services. Greenspan differed from other psychoanalytic clinicians in that he did not focus on the parent's past experiences but instead concentrated on the parent/infant maladaptive fit (Greenspan, 1981).

Contemporary child pioneers

Edward Tronick

Central to Tronick's research is the integration of mutual and self-regulation. Tronick (1989) argued that initially the infant needs to regulate physiologic states such as hunger, sleep, and activity cycles. However following close behind this accomplishment the infant then must learn to regulate affective states. All regulation is accomplished between two people and is "based on the micro-exchange of information through perceptual systems and affective displays as they are appreciated and responded to by mother and infant over time" (Stern et al., 1998, p. 907). Tronick states that self-regulation and mutual regulation occur simultaneously. He explains that the same interactive repertoire with which the infant uses to maintain and repair interactions also perform self-regulating functions (Gianino & Tronick, 1988).

Tronick collected his experimental data on self and mutual regulation by way of the "still face" experiment (Tronick et al., 1978). In this experiment after two minuets of interactive play the mother is instructed to remain in the infant's sight without moving her facial expressions, in other words, she remains dead-faced and unresponsive. When the mother presents her still-face, the well-adapted infant continues to signal the mother by smiling and making sounds while the less-adapted infant will turn to self-comforting behaviors and may withdraw and become disorganized (Tronick, 1989). Tronick's still-face experiment led him to the view that while there are always disruptions it is the repair that is crucial. His data showed that even after the mother returns to her normal self the baby's disturbed mood continues. Tronick concludes that "this finding suggests that even three month old infants are not simply under the control of the immediate stimulus situation, but that events have lasting effects, e.g., are internally represented" (Tronick, 1989, p. 114).

Studies of depressed mothers show that disruptions without repair are common in depressed mother-infant dyads. It is then that the balance between self- and mutual regulation becomes unstable (Tronick, 1989). Tronick further states that when self-regulation becomes the overwhelming job of the infant, psychopathology is a likely outcome. Tronick added that misregulation patterns set the stage for all further interactions and relationships. The infant begins to expect disruption without repair, which in turn organizes further interactions (Tronick, 1989).

Tronick's research on disruption and repair in the mother-infant dyad has led to predictions as to the "future course of the quality of the infant's attachment to his mother" (Beebe & Lachmann, 1994, p. 144). Tronick's findings aid in the knowledge of the value of the availability of the caretaker. That consistency and predictability of the object produces an organizing process. In addition to the value in understanding and predicting attachment styles the disruption and repair model has had "wide-ranging influence on psychoanalytic theories of internalization and structure formation" (Beebe & Lachmann, 1994, p. 145).

Tronick has suggested that in mutual regulation, each partner affects the other's "state of consciousness". He states: "each individual is a self-organizing system, which creates its own states of consciousness-states of brain organization-which can be expanded into more coherent and complex states in collaboration with another self-organizing system" (Tronick, 1996, p. 9 in Beebe & Lachmann, 1998). Tronick's development of the disruption-and-repair model has had a tremendous impact on the evolution of psychoanalytic theory. For example, several influential theorists such as Freud (1917e), Kline (1967), and Kohut (1971) all discuss the effect of disruption and disequilibrium as major contributors to structural organization (Beebe, Lachmann, & Jaffe, 1997).

Tronick's findings have technique implications as we come to understand that "both analyst and patient create and transform unique dyadic states of consciousness through mutual and self-regulation" (Beebe & Lachmann, 1998, p. 491). Making use of Tronick's concepts, the analyst attends to the patient's self-regulating behaviors. Without an understanding of this concept the patient's behaviors may be misjudged as evasive or dissociative.

Tronick's research on self and mutual regulation, and disruption and repair has had exceptional implications in understanding the pathology that results when the infant is faced with a chronically depressed mother. His research has furthered psychoanalytic understanding of the patient-analyst dyad and aids our understanding of what cures. In addition, Tronick's work has set the stage for other researchers to expand on his work.

Beatrice Beebe

Beatrice Beebe addressed Tronick's work on self and mutual regulation and took it one step further. She examined patterns of mutual regulation between mothers and their infants. She filmed these interactions, and slowed down the film making microanalyses possible. Beebe stated that patterns are seen. Beebe has conceptualized the various ways of interrelating and suggests "the dynamic process of reciprocal adjustments is the substance of these earliest interactive representations" (Beebe & Lachmann, 1988, p. 305). Tronick focused his work on self and mutual interactions, while Beebe's research explores mother-infant interaction. Her data helps us to understand the developing self and other representations in the infant (Beebe & Lachmann, 1988). Beebe studied normal mothers and infants (aged three to four months) at play. The baby is placed in an infant seat with the mother facing her infant. The mother and infant are left to play alone as they are filmed using the split-screen technique. This specific research examines social interactions during periods of alert attention (Beebe & Lachmann, 1988, p. 312). By slowing down the film the researcher is able to observe interactions between the mother and infant that are not visible to the naked eye. Beebe developed a scale that described the subtle variations of facial expressions that the infant and mother used to interact. Beebe revealed through these films that the mother and infant live in a "split-second" world. Beebe states: "These split-second mutual adjustments are so rapid that the temporal relations, and many of the fleeting behaviors themselves cannot be fully grasped with the naked eye." (Beebe & Lachmann, 1988, p. 316)

By following the direction of affective changes in the mother and infant, Beebe matched patterns that she felt provided the capability to share subjective states (Beebe & Lachmann, 1988). Beebe then proposed that these "interaction structures are represented over the early months of life and play a major role in the emerging symbolic forms of self- and object representations" (Beebe & Lachmann, 1988, p. 326). Beebe further argues that "characteristic patterns of self and interactive regulation form early interaction structures, which provide an important basis for emerging self and object representations" (Beebe, Lachmann, & Jaffe, 1997, p. 133). She defines interactive structures as distinguishing patterns as the different ways that mother and infant impact on one another, in other ways "patterns of the ways the interaction unfolds" (Beebe, Lachmann, & Jaffe, 1997, p. 134). Unlike other researchers, Beebe and her colleagues examined the dyad not just the individual infant. Beebe stated that by looking at the interaction between the dyad, the researcher views the information that is sent and received by both the mother and the infant simultaneously (Beebe, Lachmann, & Jaffe, 1997). Beebe's valuable research demonstrates that there is a very early organizing process that occurs as ways of relating become laid down and stable which in turn have important consequences for further development.

In another research project Beebe explored distressed infant-mother interactions. Beebe defined her theory of interaction as examining how "each partner is affected by his own behavior, self-regulation, as well as how each partner is affected by the behavior of the other" (Beebe, 2000, p. 421). She explored how maternal impingement, which causes infant withdrawal, occurs within a co-constructed process. Beebe analyzed split second videos that showed that "regardless of whether the interaction was positive or disturbed, each person's behavior could be used to predict that of the other, second by second" (Beebe, 2000, p. 423). Beebe proposed that all individuals are always trying to self-regulate in relation to what is going on in the environment. This occurs within an interactive process within the dyad. One of Beebe's most important points is that it is "not the presence of disruptions, but the balance between disruption and repair" (Beebe, 2000, p. 426). She postulated that when repairs are made after disruptions occur, the infant is more likely to be securely attached.

Beebe's findings have added to the understanding of the emerging self of the neonate making it almost impossible to continue to view the infant as undifferentiated. She has demonstrated that the earliest interactive patterns are represented pre-symbolically. "The infant forms expectations of how these interactions go, whether they are positive or negative. They organize the infant's brain, and they set up a trajectory for development." (Beebe, 2000, p. 437) Like Parens, Beebe makes use of her theoretical findings clinically. She teaches the parent to be a "baby-watcher" demonstrating how each person's behavior affects the other. Beebe encourages the parent to speak of their own childhood attempting to "link the stories of the presenting complaints, the video interaction, and the childhood history" (Beebe, 2000, p. 433). Beebe has developed her own clinical interventions. For example, when the infant presents as gaze avoidant she teaches the mother to do vocal rhythm coordination. This technique helps the infant to engage (Beebe, 2000). Even though Beebe's research is based on mothers and their infants she argues that her findings are relevant to work with adults. She claims that her research documents the slightest variation in self-object interactive regulation patterns. Beebe states: "Observing and owning this process enriches our range and flexibility as analyst. Attention to this self and interactive interface is critical to restoring, expanding, and in some cases, creating access to inner experience as well as interpersonal engagement." (Beebe, 2000, p. 510)

Alexandra Harrison

Alexandra Harrison is a pioneer in her brilliant use of film. She has taken it out of the research laboratory and brought her camera directly into the treatment room where she is able to watch in microseconds the dance between the analyst, the mother and child, and/or the interactions of a family. In our field we are used to hearing about a case as the analyst describes it; Harrison gives us the unique opportunity (when she presents her work) of being not only invited into the room, but invited to watch the back and forth as each individual responds, rejects, repairs, or reflects on the other's words, facial expressions, sounds, and movements. Harrison and Tronick (2011) call these "polysemic bundles", which many psychoanalysts do not often think about because these things occur simultaneously and in real time. Harrison emphasizes that the benefit of film is being able to repeatedly watch it slowed down into microseconds and pick up what is missed in the moment. Viewing the film segments "allows one to uncover key verbal and nonverbal interactions" (Harrison, 2005, p. 128).

Through her use of microanalysis of video, Harrison describes the "something more" than interpretation that brings about therapeutic change (Stern et al., 1998). Using infant observational research data, she adds to psychoanalytic theory and technique by suggesting, "infants interact with caregivers on the basis of a great deal of relational knowledge" (Stern et al., 1998). Infant research has demonstrated that infants anticipate and have expectations, showing surprise and a great deal of upset when expectations are not met (Stern et al., 1998). Through interactive experiences, the infant builds "adaptive strategies ... [that] constitute the initial organization of his/her domain of *implicit relational knowing*" (Stern et al., 1998). Stern and Harrison point out that *implicit relational knowing* is not reserved for the pre-verbal/pre-symbolic infant, but that all of us interact on this level, including the therapist/patient dyad within the transference. They call this "the 'shared implicit moment' ... with its roots in the earliest relationships" (Stern et al., 1998).

Harrison has developed the parent consultation model (PCM) using microanalysis of videos of family meetings "as the basis for formulations concerning the child's psychological problems" (Harrison, 2005, p. 129). PCM is based on developmental theory, making use of microanalysis of filmed interactions to offer a clinical "assessment of relationship, the mother-child relationship, the sibling relationship, and the marital relationship" (Harrison, 2005, p. 137). Harrison states: "time spent in the family session is short, but videotaped transcription makes possible the recognition of repeated patterns on a micro level, contributing to the larger level behaviors that constitute an adaptation" (Harrison, 2005, p. 138).

James Herzog

James Herzog proposes a theoretical concept, triadic reality, which he defines as "interacting representations of self with mother, self with father, and self with mother and father" (Herzog, 2005, p. 1,030). In order for this to happen, the parents must be "lovers, friends, and co-participants in a parenting alliance" (Herzog, 2005, p. 1,032). Herzog states that triadic reality is a necessary structural accomplishment that is essential for entering into the Oedipal phase of development. If triadic reality is not sufficiently navigated, the Oedipal phase will have a problematic resolution and cause future difficulties in development.

Herzog further claims that when children lack "self-with-mother-and-father-together" a narcissistic fixation occurs and these children have a higher probability of developing narcissistic personality disorder (Herzog, 2004). Herzog states, "the introduction of psychoanalytic intervention for such children has a high degree of therapeutic success, as new representations are constructed that mirror actual interactions" (Herzog, 2005, p. 1,031). Herzog further postulates that when the mother demeans the father and contempt enters the relationship, the child is predisposed to narcissistic pathology (Herzog, 2004).

Herzog, a luminous and talented child analyst, has the ability to provide and co-create with all of his patients a play space and then to share this creative experience with the rest of us. This is truly a gift as very few analysts as exceptional as Herzog are willing to share their work so intimately. When one reads Herzog or listens to his presentations, it is better than being a fly on the wall, it is as if the listener joins in with both the patient and analyst and becomes part of the experience. Part of this is Herzog's ability to tell his stories both in the written word and verbal presentation, but I believe it is mostly his talent in being able to connect and play with his patients on a deep and intimate level.

Moving beyond theoretical history

The history of child psychoanalysis tells the story of its growth and evolution along with its controversies. The *real* story of child psychoanalysis is told within the walls of the treatment room where the work between analyst and child patient takes place. The following analytic treatments of six children demonstrate the value of child analysis that has been handed down, beginning with Hug-Hellmuth and moving on to Anna Freud and Melanie Klein, and all the child analysts who have followed.

PART I

SEVERE PSYCHOPATHOLOGY

CHAPTER TWO

The autistic child

Leo Kanner (1943) characterized infantile autism as an innate disturbance in affect that obstructed social relationships and hindered language development. In addition, children who suffered from autism were unable to play symbolically and seemed to be intolerant of change (Kanner, 1943). These children who seemed to disappear into their own world became a challenge to psychoanalysts who wondered if these children had "an internal world that they could not express, that they isolated themselves from others because of an intolerable hypersensitivity to sound or human contact" (Bergman & Escalona, 1949, p. 333). It was an unfortunate occurrence that within the diagnosis of infantile autism mothers of these challenging children was described as "icebox mothers" and were blamed for their children's disorder. It was not long until parents began to feel accused and blamed resulting in negative feelings toward the psychotherapists and psychiatrists who they hoped would help them (Shapiro, 2000).

In the past, psychoanalytic theory and practice has been understood and taught with little reference to neurobiology. It is assumed that the individual is responsible for one's own inner life. The past two-plus decades have demonstrated that "neuroscience accounts of body/brain/mind linkages (Shore, 1994) are now being added to more familiar nexus of experience/phantasy/mind" (Shuttleworth, 1999, p. 240). Recent neurobiological research states that there are several neurobiological problems that "interface with the social brain and therefore lead to autism" (Singletary, 2012, p. 1). For example: a research study using fMRIs with high-functioning adolescents with autistic spectrum disorder (ASD) compared to normal adolescents showed considerable "decreases in connectivity between three regions of the social brain in those with ASD" (Gotts et al., 2012 in Singletary, 2012). The greater the decreases in connectivity, the more severe social impairment was found (Gotts et al., 2012).

ASD is understood as a compilation of symptoms that develop because of a fundamental yet diverse neurological deficit in emotional communication and information processing. It appears that the atypical brain configuration seen in children with ADS is attributed to various factors such as genetics, as well as pre-and perinatal developmental influences (Klin, McPartland, & Volkmar, 2005). ADS secondary defenses arise against feelings experienced as a result of these deficits. In addition, because of these neurological limitations and their related psychological defenses, the child with ASD lacks social experiences and frequently experiences traumatic interactions where she is rejected again and again (Allured, 2006; Bromfield, 1989).

As with all children, the progress of the ADS child's development depends on her environment as well as her biology. It is known that there is a broad range in the severity of the biological predisposition to autism and that early interactions with caregivers may determine how well the infant develops. For example: "some children may be born so disabled that parents, however healthily nurturing, make limited impact. Whereas other children may be born with a milder innate vulnerability, but encounter significantly damaging parents." (Bromfield, 1989, p. 447)

Asperger syndrome

Hans Asperger (1944), a Viennese pediatrician, described four boys who demonstrated characteristic developmental differences in spite of high intelligence and adequate language ability. All of the boys had significant trouble with social interactions, demonstrating a limited capacity in understanding the mind of the other (Asperger, 1944). Asperger syndrome (AS) is seen by some to be a personality or character type that is clearly distinct from ASD (Van Krevelen, 1971; Wing, 1991; Hodges, 2004; Simpson, 2004), while others propose that AS is on a diagnostic spectrum with autism (Shapiro, 2000; Frith, 2004; Klin et al., 2005). The most recent studies show that AS is a form of high-functioning autism with the same biological determinants (Cohler & Weiner, 2011). As with ASD, AS is understood by many to be based on multifaceted interactions between genetics and developmental neurobiology (Folstein & Santangelo, 2000; Rutter, 2005; Lincoln et al., 1998; Schultz et al., 2000; Minshew et al., 2005). AS is associated with genetic factors that combine with pre-or postnatal difficulties; however, studies show that neurological findings have been inconclusive and inconsistent regarding neurological pathology (Gillberg & Ehlers, 1998; Klin et al., 2005). Children with AS have difficulty assimilating experiences into a coherent narrative of their world (Frith, 1991). Cohler and Weiner describe these children as "having difficulty in being able to understand others, in engaging in pretend play, and in using imagination. These patients have particular difficulty in being able to predict or explain others' intentions. Other people remain an enigma that creates anxiety and uncertainty." (Cohler & Weiner, 2011, p. 212)

It is well known that psychoanalysis is not considered to be the recommended treatment for children on the autistic spectrum, even among psychoanalysts (Sugarman, 2011). Sugarman states several reasons for this. To begin with, in the 1960s Bettelheim claimed that a disorder that had a biological component could not be helped by a psychodynamic approach. In recent years it has become generally accepted that autism is a developmental disorder with a neurobiological origin. This conviction has led to an abandonment of psychodynamic treatment in favor of behavioral methods that teach and train the child (Bromfield, 2000). The belief that psychodynamic treatment is of little value in a neurologically based disorder disregards recent research and clinical data that "emotional experience can facilitate the development of brain structure and function, which can, in turn, make it possible to manage even quite severe deficits" (Rhode & Klauber, 2004, p. 267).

In addition, psychoanalysis privileges verbal interpretation focusing on the development of insight into ones' unconscious. Sugarman states: "deciphering the unconscious meaning of the patient's verbalizations ignores the problem that Asperger's patients have with mentalizing or developing a theory of mind" (Sugarman, 2011, p. 222). He urges us to not allow the character defenses that arise to help manage such incapacitating deficits to "not obscure the essential constitutional basis of the patient's difficulties even though, of course, such limitations will become components of compromise formations" (Sugarman, 2011, p. 222). As mentioned by Sugarman, patients with ASD struggle to understand their own mind and the mind of the other, a facility known as mentalizing and/or a theory of mind (Atwood, 2007; Fonagy, 2008; Hodges, 2004). Psychoanalytic, psychodynamic therapy underscores the realization of insight within the empathic "holding environment" between the patient and the analyst. Within the therapeutic space the individual with ASD is able to expand her awareness of her therapist's mind as well as her own mind and becomes better able to mentalize. However, in working with ASD patients, action and interaction are required. Sugarman stresses that while "verbal interpretations, although remaining important, become no more privileged than any other intervention that promotes the Asperger's patient's capacity for insightfulness" (Sugarman, 2011, p. 228).

A primary goal of the treatment with a patient with Asperger syndrome is to facilitate the development of insight, by providing a safe space where the patient learns new skills through her interactions with the analyst. Within this frame, while understanding and utilizing transference in its broadest sense, the patient begins to reflect on and become aware of her inner life. As the patient and analyst co-construct a space in which the patient experiences the therapist's efforts to understand her, she may begin to see that allowing oneself to get to know the mind of the other does not have to be frightening. Within this frame the analyst and patient create a play space, which is essential to development of imagination and creativity (Cohler & Weiner, 2011). Sugarman reminds us, "all patients demonstrate both symbolic and nonsymbolic mental functioning and hence all patients will need an analytic treatment that focuses on promoting mentalization. Asperger's is just as potentially analyzable as any other patient." (Sugarman, 2011, 225). Autism spectrum disorder is a neurodevelopmental disorder with psychological and behavioral consequences, which are potentially treatable (Singletary, 2012).

The case of Helen

Sixteen-year-old Helen came into treatment in an unconventional way. She had recently been released by the hospital after a forty-eight-hour stay. She had gone to the ER on her own as an attempt to demand that her parents take notice of her distress. Helen had become despondent because of a perceived rejection by her uncle for whom she had formed an attachment. Helen was extremely demanding of his attention, sometimes calling over 100 times in an evening, leaving frantic messages for him to return her calls. He explained to her that his own family and children took precedence over her; therefore he could only speak with her occasionally. Helen construed this interaction to mean that he did not care for her and she experienced it as a devastating rejection. In the hospital she was prescribed anti-psychotic medication, told she was probably bipolar, and released with instructions to see a psychiatrist.

Helen had a plan; her uncle had described his own personal analytic treatment to her. She became intrigued and was determined to pursue an analysis for herself. Helen read a little about Freud and searched the internet until she located me through our institute's referral service. She required an analyst who was within walking distance of her high school. In our initial phone conversation she explained her financial situation and her need for a low fee. She was determined to pay for it herself, afraid that neither of her parents would help her. Helen was emphatic that she could not rely on them to financially or emotionally support her treatment.

In her first several sessions, Helen appeared disturbed with her head turned down and away from me, looking only at the floor. She was unable to risk sneaking even the tiniest glance at me. She wore an over-sized sweatshirt over torn, dirty black pants that were her uniform for many months to come. Her hair was a stringy mess, and her movements were extremely awkward. I was not at all sure that I wanted to treat her or if I could help her, but Helen *demanded* an analysis. She was determined to find a way out from her pain, a way to alleviate her tormented life. I was struck by her resiliency and her astounding tenacity in spite of remarkable ineptness and difficulties being in the world. With apprehension I agreed to begin an intensive analytic treatment, uncertain as to where our turbulent journey together would take us.

History

Helen was the second of three children. She was born when her older sister was three. Her mother became pregnant with her brother when she was two months old. Her mother was not college educated and from Helen's description and memories, she was depressed and overwhelmed. She spent long afternoons locked in her bedroom while the three children ate candy and watched television. Helen's father was a professional who worked long hours and was unavailable to his family. Helen's childhood memories are of verbal and physical fighting, harsh punishment, isolation, and being told she was "retarded" and "crazy". She was unable to read until fourth grade and was assigned to a special education classroom. She remembered feeling enraged all the time. In school she would act out by jumping from desktop to desktop screaming all the while. At home she would fight with her siblings and parents and hurt neighborhood children. For example, she would ride her bike very fast through a group of small children with the intention of harming them.

Her father told Helen that her mother was depressed after her birth and too tired and weak to care for both a new baby and a three-year-old. In addition, she became pregnant with her little brother when Helen was only two months old. Her father would often find Helen crying in her crib in a soiled diaper at the end of the day, obviously left alone for several hours unattended. Helen's mother would be asleep, while her sister ate junk food and watched television, also unattended.

I speculate that Helen's mother had her own severe limitations. Helen described her as learning disabled and stupid. From Helen's descriptions of both of her parents, it seems possible that they both show signs of idiosyncratic modes of thinking and behaving. Both parents appeared to have difficulties in relating to others. Klin et al. (2005) review several studies that point to a genetic influence among children with AS: "these patients have been reported to have close relatives, particularly fathers, with some of the same character style as AS patients" (Cohler & Weiner, 2011, p. 213).

When Helen was nine years old her mother became romantically involved with a man she had met on the internet. When Helen was twelve years old her parents divorced and her mother moved to another state with her lover. Her mother had no other friends. Two years later her mother gave birth to another daughter and a year later was diagnosed with fourth stage breast cancer. She died when Helen was nineteen years old. Helen's childhood memories were of her mother spending long hours in her bathroom and bedroom behind a locked door. Helen's mother seemed to have a disturbed relationship with her own mother. Helen described her maternal grandmother as a nasty, mean old lady who was verbally abusive and physically intrusive. Helen remembered being shamed for defecating in her diaper and being cleaned in a physically rough fashion by her grandmother.

Bergman writes that mothers of autistic babies are often "doubly traumatized, first by the deprivation of their relationships to their own mothers and then by the profound frustration and disappointment of not being able to be a good mother" (Bergman, 2000, p. 63). It is impossible to know a great deal about Helen's first year, other than what her father told her, but I speculate that infant Helen was unable to accept the little emotional sustenance her mother was able to provide her. It is possible that a combination of Helen's "impaired social information processing, cognition, empathic accuracy, and social motivation" (Singletary, 2012) negatively impacted on her experience of and her ability to have loving, comforting relationships, which in turn hindered her sense of wellbeing (Singletary, 2012).

I imagine that Helen was easily over-stimulated and overwhelmed causing a gross misattunement between mother and infant. One could easily envision Helen as a baby unable to be comforted, perhaps stiffening when held and averting her eyes from her mother's gaze. Because of her neurobiological deficits, Helen may have reacted to her mother's attempts to comfort her by anxiety and a sense of threat (Mahler, 1968). Helen's mother did not have the support or the knowledge to begin to understand Helen's differences and limitations. It is easy to imagine that she turned away from her infant daughter in an effort to fend off her own devastating feelings of failure and rejection. Bergman states: "that the psychotic child blocks the mother's capacity to enter into this special state of motherhood" (Bergman, 2000, p. 63). It is possible that Helen misinterpreted loving gestures from her mother as frightening, which in turn caused her to turn inward. Singletary states: "the child's efforts to make sense of and cope with the experience of aloneness and danger could lead to a defensive withdrawal from others and to psychological conflicts regarding relationships" (Singletary, 2012). Patterns of maladaptive interactions are set into motion as the infant attempts to protect herself from overwhelming, frightening affects as she misinterprets her mother's intentions to comfort her. In Helen's case, I speculate that her mother's own limitations were an added factor that combined with Helen's neurological complications set up a "pathway leading to the various clinical manifestations

of the syndrome of ASD, both in its development and maintenance"
(Singletary, 2012, p. 7).

First three years of analysis

*I remember when I was four years old. I was staring out the window and had a
weird feeling … like something was missing … that I was missing something,
and I felt ashamed.*

For the first month, Helen sat up facing me with her head either
turned to the side or down, stealing a glance at me upon entering the
room, but never when leaving. She spoke endlessly of great shame,
degrading her body and all things female: *I hate my arms and thighs …
my hips. I don't want anyone to look at me. I can't trust anyone. I am afraid I
will be harmed or raped. I feel disgusted.*

I asked her about the feeling of disgust stating that it was a very
strong emotion. Helen did not respond directly to my statement but
continued:

*My mother hated my body and how I looked. My father hates women. They
are weak and ugly. Women are very ugly and disgusting. I can't lose weight.
If I did boys would want me they would look at me and I would be raped. My
mother had an affair and they had sex and I heard them. It was creepy. I had
breasts when I was eight years old. I hid them. I hated them and would tie
tape around them to make them flat. I got my period when I was ten. My mom
was not open about these things. I had no idea what was happening to me.
She embarrassed me and made me wipe myself and show her the blood. I felt
disgusted.*

Helen claimed that she did not possess feelings and when I pointed
out that she was describing a feeling she denied their existence ada-
mantly. In Helen's mind, the emotion was put on her from the outside
world, from her environment.

After a few weeks of describing hateful feelings toward women,
she began to describe her early school years: *When I was in kindergarten
I remember watching the other kids as if I was invisible. It felt dark … I couldn't
be with them and when I tired they didn't want me. I was the most unpopular
kid in the school. I just went crazy. I wouldn't learn.*

It is an underlying problem that children with AS experience the world
as indifferent and insensitive (Topel & Lachmann, 2008). A few weeks
later she recalled a dream where she beat her uncle and grandmother's
dog with a bat. It felt visceral, filled with primitive rage. After telling

me this dream she abruptly stated that she could not bear sitting across from me any longer and lay down on my couch. I was not sure this was a good idea but also felt she needed to be relieved of the pressure of facing me. Once she was no longer facing me, her rage became volcanic. Helen berated her father, her mother, her siblings, her uncle, her grandmother, her teachers, and just about everyone she had ever come in contact with. Her stories were very sad as she always ended up the victim. It was clear that her object relations were severely compromised. My empathic responses to her pain and suffering did not bring relief but instead seemed to elicit more rageful outbursts. She herself did not seem to feel empathy for anyone or anything.

Helen began to direct her rage toward me; for example, she watched the clock and if I was even a minute late she spent her full session berating me for stealing time away from her and giving it to the previous patient. Helen described that as soon as I was even a second late it was proof that I had forgotten about her and she became furious. She was determined to prove that I did not like her and was trying to get rid of her, and could not hold her in mind. She complained about my office stating that it was ugly: my art was ugly, my chairs were ugly, and I was the ugliest woman she had ever seen. I began to dread her appointments and would brace myself taking a deep breath in order to face the onslaught of her fury. She screamed at me for well over two years. There were many times she made me furious and I would find myself wishing we had never begun, and a few times I lost my temper and shot sharp words in her direction. However, these ruptures were repaired, which was an entirely new experience for Helen. For the most part I kept my analytic composure, made interpretations when I thought appropriate, and provided a safe place for her to scream at me or whomever I represented on that particular day. Sugarman points out that "our own countertransference feelings and actions alert us to something in the interaction that we want to point out to the patient" (Sugarman, 2011, p. 228). My goal with Helen during this difficult period was to withstand her violent storms, remain attuned to her sense of worthlessness, and somehow begin to help her become mindful, in other words, to begin to know her own mind and the mind of the other. I interpreted that she could only feel close to me through rage, and she was showing me what it was like growing up in her home and that was beyond horrendous!

Weekend separations became difficult for Helen and she began to call and scream into my message machine. When I returned her calls she would not allow me to end the call. This behavior was a reenactment of a screen memory where, as a very small child, she would cling to her mother's leg insisting on attention that only came through angry words, spankings, and abandonment when her mother retreated behind a locked door to avoid her daughter's demands. We solved this problem by using email. In this way Helen could stay connected to me outside of session times and I did not feel overly intruded upon. Helen continues to email me but no longer needs immediate replies or even, at times, a reply at all.

Helen developed a shameful secret desire to know more about me but could never ask in a forthright manner. It took her a long time to confess that she had searched for and found an article on the internet about my daughter, who at the time was a well-established professional ballet dancer. This knowledge provoked tremendous malignant envy in Helen. She defended against her sense of worthlessness by defiling my daughter (and me in the process) and exhibiting extreme grandiosity. It is interesting to note that AS in children and adolescents "bears some striking similarities to narcissistic personality disorder" (Shuttleworth, 1999, p. 239). The narcissistic patient's inability to form intimate long-lasting relationships is understood as motivated by envy, anxiety, and aggression. The AS patient will often be filled with envy, contend with severe anxiety, and be overwhelmed with hostile aggression, but must also cope with neurobiological deficiencies.

Around this same time Helen became concerned that I might retire or die. When I suggested that she was fearful that her anger and envy would kill me either by me kicking her out, or in her fantasy, really die, she confessed that she had been, and at times, continued to be physically hurtful to animals by kicking, hitting, and pulling tails. Helen stated:

I have a very cold heart. It's hard to be nice to people. My heart is very cold, my heart feels evil. I do good things because I am supposed to. It never comes from my heart. I am mean and I make people upset on purpose. I used to think my heart was made of stone because my father always said he didn't have a heart and he was proud of that. I hated everybody, nobody would help me and when they tried they only harmed me. I got everything wrong. When I was in first grade I couldn't even count. I felt stupid, everyone hated me so I hated them back. Girls were mean to me and my mother taught me ways to get back at them, to get my revenge.

Nobody played with me. My only friends were my hands. My right hand would beat up my left hand. I would talk to my hands, they were my only friends.

Dream: [Before telling me her dream she needed to apologize for her feelings, worried I would be angry and reject her for her unconscious fantasies about me.] *You were dying, terminally ill. You were dying of cancer but you had ten years to live but ten years of suffering.* [She smiled a cruel sneer as she told me her dream, and began to laugh anxiously.]

Helen's worries were that I would leave her and betray her as she felt her uncle had done. No matter how I responded to her she felt criticized, unheard, and misunderstood. She could not tolerate my silence nor could she tolerate my words. I slowly began to show her how she misinterpreted my words and my intentions and how this is what has happened to her throughout her whole life.

Helen continued to have dreams almost nightly where I either left her or hurt her in some way until: *I dreamed that I was alone in the dark and you helped me get home.* Around this time Helen was able to apply for, and get a job in food service where she met a boy who appeared to also be on the spectrum and they became a couple. Several months later Helen became sexually active. She hated kissing, describing it as disgusting, and felt numb and dead when having sex. Her relationship was tumultuous as she always felt he was hurting her or not doing enough for her. She turned her rage away from me (for the time being) and her passive, innocent boyfriend became the vessel to be filled with her hate. When I pointed out her nasty, hurtful actions she felt victorious and justified in her hate and rage, because it was proof that I did not care for her but preferred her boyfriend and took his side.

Helen's mother's cancer metastasized and her death seemed imminent. She blamed her mother for not taking proper care of herself and claimed that she would die young but she should have at least another five to ten years. When I attempted to insert some reality into this situation she snapped: *I don't want to talk about my mother, she isn't worth my time! I want to talk about me!* Helen moved back with her father, sister and brother, graduated from high school, and found an analyst (with my help) for her boyfriend. She began to obsess about germs and disease as she worried about every ache and pain and became hysterical when she found she had to have a cavity repaired; yet she was lax with her personal hygiene. She ranted about old people (afraid I was old enough to retire) describing them as smelling of death. She was terrified of becoming ill because of her fear of vomiting. Helen was sure she would die if she vomited.

She began college filled with fears that she would fail while simultaneously defending against these fears with grandiose fantasies, her narcissism suffocating us both.

> **Dream:** *I am having a session but it is in my bed and I was holding your hand and feeling very close to you, but then I saw bugs and started to squirm.*
>
> **Associations:** *I hate bugs.*
>
> A: *You were feeling close, you allowed us to be close but it became uncomfortable and ugly, perhaps a way to get away from the close feelings.*

Even though Helen continued her rages and often spoke of not trusting me and feeling nothing for me, her dreams/unconscious told another story as I continued to interpret her narcissistic defenses against allowing us to experience intimacy.

She became disillusioned with her boyfriend because he was so empty and could not hold an interesting conversation and broke up with him. In this particular session she stated that she had a desire to look at me and turned her head toward me behind the couch and quickly turned away covering her face with her sweatshirt. *This couch is my safety zone; your hallway is safe too, but not the doorway.* I wondered about her use of the couch as a resistance, but kept that thought to myself. Her conflict of her wish to be close to me surfaced in an action when she confessed with great shame that she now had proof that I was a bad person because she searched the court system and discovered I had been divorced.

H: *I wanted to find something really bad and I did. Happy people don't get divorced. Normal people don't get divorced. It was aggressive of me. I wanted to hurt you. I don't want to know where you live. I don't want to think that you have a life outside of this office. I don't want to share you with anyone. I hate your other patients.*

Helen spoke about her dying mother who was bald and had no breasts: *She just complains all the time. She isn't even female anymore. I feel more female because she isn't anymore. It helps me feel more female. It's pretty bad. She can't do anything. She's dying and it isn't a quick death. It's hard to watch. She did this to herself and now she is dying and can't be there for me.*

Dream: *There is a bunny on my mother's chest kneading her breasts like a kitten trying to get milk. I woke up really sad.*

Dream: *I was in here and there were a lot of college students in here. I hate sharing you. I was angry and sad at the same time. You were ignoring me. I left and came back in wearing a girly dress like a ballerina and lie on the couch and fall asleep and had a dream where I make eye contact with you and you look younger. You were proud of me and we hug and you kiss the top of my head. But I wake up and you tell me it was only a dream. You leave and I feel rejected. I lost my time. You gave it to the college students.*

Helen wants desperately to feel close to me but confesses that if she allows herself to feel close it becomes sexual and that is too shameful and disgusting. She also feels I could not possibly reciprocate the feelings and that would be too painful. The feelings of shame that dominated her early months of analysis return full force and everything becomes shameful. She divulges that she binge eats and her oral desires become the most shameful of all. Helen becomes *numb* and *dead* in an effort to avoid shameful humiliation until one day she experiences guilt. She cries: *The sadness is pouring out of me. I am so sorry for all the bad things I have done. I feel so bad for hurting everyone and being so mean. I feel so guilty!!!!*

Helen's mother died while I was on vacation. She claimed that she felt nothing, but the weeks following her mother's death were filled with angry acting-out behaviors. Eventually her anger began to subside and she began to allow herself to feel sad, and began to feel empathy for others. After speaking about her little sister's plight of being left motherless at age three-and-a-half, she said: *The more I feel less angry, the more I can empathize with little children, the more sad I get that I had such a sad childhood.*

As her third year of analysis progresses we work more intensely on how she often misreads and misinterprets our interactions. This made her furious and was narcissistically injurious, but I felt was necessary for her to move forward in her treatment. For example, Helen brought in a photo of herself with her little sister. After I spent a few minutes examining the photograph I made several comments about her little sister. She became furious and began to rant: *You took more time looking at her. I am unimportant! I just don't care about you! You don't get me and you never will!*

I commented how she was testing me and set me up to fail so she could prove how terrible I am and worthless to her. She exclaimed: *I don't have trouble reading people, I just expect people to treat me badly!* It is clear that Helen has "significant impairments in key mental functions like mentalizing, affect regulation, self and object representational capacity, and social language" (Sugarman, 2011, p. 224), and when I attempted to explore her fears and fantasies, or understand symbolic significance of her thoughts and behaviors, she often became confused and enraged, attacking me in response to my efforts.

The following took place two months later, after breaking up with her boyfriend yet again.

H: *When I was driving here I saw E. He didn't see me. He is dopey. I'm not going to talk to him for another three months. He doesn't get it. When I'm with him I feel bad about myself. I feel bad about my body. That makes me hate him. Makes me feel really bad. I get mean to him. I am always mean to him and he is always the victim.*

A: *I wonder why that happens? Do you think it has anything to do with feeling close?*

H: *The feelings I have in here with you are different. The feelings for him are sexual not close.*

At this point she asked if she could move off of the couch and sit up but was unable to look at me. We spoke about the use of the couch and Helen felt that the couch was not allowing her to feel close to me and she was using it as a resistance. As she was leaving she said: *You seem more real.*

Helen has remained sitting up. It was painfully difficult for her to meet my gaze, and this caused her great shame. At this point I was able to interpret that because her needs were not met as a baby and young child, these same needs feel shameful. Eventually over several months she was able to maintain eye contact and felt very guilty for calling me names in the past and for thinking *evil thoughts.*

At the end of her third year of analysis Helen wrote and gave to me the following paragraph:

I was born with Autism, and I know no other way of being. Imagine living your life in a skewed reality. You walk into a room and try your hardest to make sense of what is going on and what others are thinking. You have to consciously *think about what expression you are wearing on your face and what you **should** be feeling. Everything is confusing. When people talk you need to figure out how to interpret what they mean, but it is impossible because your brain just won't let you. You see this happening every time someone says something and you just can't figure it out. You can't read their facial expressions or social cues and are trying to think of what to say. And when you try to talk, your words come out confusing and unclear, and may not have much to do with what they just said. Every single day is a struggle. There is no escape. There is a longing that I feel to bond with others and I die on the inside when I realize that it just is not working. Invisible tears fill me up inside. Right now it is hard to imagine my life being able to connect well with others. I have improved in the last three years. I can connect a little bit, but it makes me so uncomfortable I cannot stop laughing. I get scared. Others can see that I am afraid. It is a very painful reality. I get rejected over and over. I keep trying. I must overcome my condition. One day I will have a friend. That is my dream.*

Years four to eight

Helen's fourth year of treatment was difficult as she attempted to coerce me into behaving in ways that she thought I should. For example, she would tell me that she missed and/or loved me and when I did not respond by matching her words she became enraged and claimed it was proof that I did not care at all about her. This would happen repeatedly in different scenarios. This period of time was followed by many weeks where she trashed our work and me. She would attempt to trap me by asking me to repeat exactly what she had said fifteen minutes earlier and when I fell short or refused to comply she would state that I was too stupid to be of any help to her and the previous years had been a waste.

As she began her fifth year of treatment she reminisced about her treatment viewing her progress while simultaneously owning the nasty, mean parts of her personality. She described how when she felt empty she became furious and would do something mean to another person such as her former boyfriend (who has remained in her life) and/or me. *If I make you feel bad or him, it makes me feel better. I feel powerful and good. I don't like that about myself.*

In the summer of her sixth year, Helen went abroad to study. We had several Skype sessions during those months. Helen was extremely disappointed in her experience because her fantasy was that people in another country would be different and would like her. This was devastating, but helped her to begin to explore her expectations of others. In some ways her relationship with me was deceiving because I was dependable, non-judgmental (for the most part), and accepting of her limitations. Her expectations of others was relentless; the second someone disappointed her she experienced the action as a narcissistic wound and disposed of the person finding the whole experience humiliating, and shameful resulting in rage and depression. This was painful for her to view and explore. When she returned she began to arrive late to her sessions and at times, stand me up. This behavior continued for four months until she came in late extremely angry that traffic had been the cause. Helen was furious with me because the night before she had begun to read the book *Necessary Losses* that I had loaned to her two years ago and had completely forgotten about. Helen was able to relate to Vorst's description of narcissistic personality disorder and saw herself in the case descriptions in the book. She also felt disgusted by Vorst's description of "bliss in the womb". The next day she tells me this dream: *I was in my house where I was a child and a robber was trying to get in and hurt me. I couldn't get out. I was trapped.* Her associations were to the metaphor of "bliss in the womb". *I have a feeling that my mother's womb was not comforting to me. Maybe I was trapped in a bad mother. She was always trying to get away from me, pushing me away when I was little. I always find relationships where this happens.* I was then able to point out how this had occurred between the two of this in the previous session.

Later course of treatment

In her eighth year of analysis, Helen continued to feel numb and *dead* at times but for the most part, was able to feel a vast array of emotions from deep sadness to playful glee. She continued to have difficulties listening to my interpretations or suggestions, as her impulse was to immediately tell me I was simply wrong, but we persevered and she continued to work hard in her treatment, never missing a session.

Helen secured a good job within her profession, and experimented with romantic relationships that usually ended within a few months. She began to view and explore her pattern of gravitating toward unavailable men, but was able to connect this with her past relationship with her mother. Helen continued to struggle with female friendships and for quite some time did not find a true friend. She remained hopeful.

Conclusion

Helen's case demonstrates how children born with a neurobiological deficit in emotional communication and information processing develop secondary defenses in order to protect one from experiencing the self as defective. Because of Helen's inborn biological deficit, and because her parents were unable to provide her with appropriate treatment, Helen lacked social experiences and was traumatized over and over through out her childhood, when other children and adults repeatedly rejected her overtures.

When Helen began her analysis she had little understanding of her own mind and was unable to understand the mind of her analyst. Over time, Helen began to trust that I would not reject her and within our therapeutic space she began to know her own mind, and to be better able to mentalize. As our relationship grew closer and Helen was able to allow herself to feel vulnerable, she began to reflect on her inner life. Within this process Helen was able to become more imaginative and creative. Helen and I weathered many storms, both intrapsychic and environmental, and over time, Helen came to trust that her aggression would neither kill me nor cause me to reject her and she no longer needed to live in a world filled with rage. I have attempted to demonstrate that young people like Helen, who are on the spectrum, are "potentially analyzable as any other patient" (Sugarman, 2011, p. 225).

CHAPTER THREE

The homeless child

others with young children are the fastest growing segment of the homeless population (Baumohl, 1996). When there is chronic stress as a result of extreme poverty and racism, how do families stay functional and cope? What happens when family structure breaks down, leaving young, single mothers alone to care for these children? What happens to parenting skills when the mother is poor, homeless, and isolated from family and community support? How do mothers parent when addicted to alcohol or drugs? The combined stress of extreme poverty and homelessness can greatly impair the ability of single mothers to parent their children effectively. A history of poor attachments and abusive relationships added to the chronic stress of poverty and homelessness may cause the mother to feel powerless and inadequate.

It has been documented that infants whose mothers are unable to provide comfort and protection and do not foster an interest in the world, will not develop the ability for self-regulation. Greenspan states that these babies show increased tendencies toward muscle rigidity, gaze aversion, and disorganized sleep and eating patterns (Greenspan, 1990). Moreover, the homeless mother is preoccupied with daily, and sometimes hourly, survival. The homeless infant may be overwhelmed, and sleep brings peace from an over stimulating and abusive environment (Koplow, 1996).

The mother without a home is unable to provide an intimate environment wherein the infant may experience her as provider and protector. The mother often feels helpless and inadequate in her ability to care for her child in terms of the most basic provision of shelter. Because she herself is totally dependent on others for survival she may defensively detach from her child's dependency needs (Koplow, 1996). Opening herself to her infant's emotional needs would require her to become reacquainted with painful experiences in the present and the past. If her experience was one of rejection and neglect it is much too painful and dangerous to *feel* in the absence of family and home. Karen states: "when one becomes a parent, unresolved pain is shaken loose, the defensive wall is breached and new defensive efforts are required" (Karen, 1998, p. 374). When a homeless mother gazes at her child, her own pain and sadness is mirrored back. Unable to bear her own painful feelings, the mother is also unable to feel empathy for her child's plight. Her new defense is to distance herself from her child. The mother's own depression and powerlessness become overwhelming. Stern calls this the "dead mother complex." He explains that the mother's depression allows her to be physically present but emotionally absent (Stern, 1995). It is easy to understand that both mother and child use most of their energy to survive.

The case of Sara

Sara spent her first four years of life homeless. Her mother (Esther) spent the first two years of motherhood pushing Sara in a stroller by day in search of a warm, safe place to sleep at night. Esther's own history is one of severe poverty, physical abuse, domestic violence, neglect, and ultimately abandonment. Her own mother was neglectful of her as a child and was murdered when Esther was a young teenager. Esther's narrative is one in which she is called *stupid* and *retarded* as far back as she can remember. She carries the labels *developmentally delayed* and *cognitively limited*. Esther tells of physical abuse at the hands of her father and was literally thrown out of her father's house by his girlfriend when Sara was one month old. As Esther sat in my office telling me "facts" about her past without visible emotion, she experienced a vivid memory. She became agitated and recalled: *It was January, I remember.*

It was January and cold [she shivers]. She put me and the baby out. I was *standing on the porch with no place to go. It was night too and really cold.* Esther looked at me (one of the few moments where she was able to maintain eye contact) in disbelief.

It was easy to imagine Esther taking off down the city streets with Sara in tow, walking quickly and with purpose. I imagine she is trying her best simultaneously to walk away from her abusive past and painful memories and walk toward a better, safer place. For two years Esther and Sara lived on the street. There was a kindly old grandfather, who offered his couch many a night, but he died; then there was nobody. When Sara was two, Esther had another baby girl. Esther was no longer able to survive on the streets with two babies. Only then did this young family enter the shelter system. I first met this young family when Sara was twenty-seven months old, as they had come to live at our shelter. Sara was recommended for individual therapy because the daycare and clinical staff were concerned that the mother/child relationship was poor. Staff members observed that Esther seemed not to "see" her daughter and was unaware of the child's emotional needs.

The initial contact

During our first session I was struck by Sara's profound sadness. Though painfully shy, she left her daycare room with me easily. It is important to note that I was a complete stranger to Sara, and she left her daycare with me without any visible anxiety of emotion. When children have not been able to develop a secure attachment in infancy they often feel little or no distress or anxiety when separation or loss of love is threatened (Freud, 1965, p. 122).

Sara presented developmentally as a twelve- to eighteen-month-old baby. Her vocabulary consisted of fewer than twenty words. I sensed that she was unaware of her own body in space; her movements were stiff and awkward. She did not notice obstacles and would trip over small toys. She stiffened when touched and it was reported by daycare staff that she would not allow other children to touch her. She cried and fought staff when they changed her diaper. For the most part, her affect was flat and she did not make eye contact. My first goal with Sara was to foster her ability to form an attachment and connect with me. I began to see her three times per week. Thus the most exhausting, heart-wrenching, yet beautiful and rewarding relationship began to develop between Sara and myself.

Early phases of our work

Our work began on the most primitive, preverbal level. I slowly began to connect with her through body movements, facial gestures, and responses and shared posture. For example, Sara discovered the sink in my office and began to pour the water in and out of a baby bottle. As she did this she made noises that I joined her, using the similar inflections in my voice, as I mirrored her facial expressions. This was the first time she made eye contact with me.

In another early session Sara found the baby lotion on my shelf and gestured for me to help pour some on her hands. She took the lotion and gingerly rubbed it into my cheek while maintaining deep eye contact. I asked her if I could put some lotion on her and began to rub some on her arm. Her affect changed from serious exploration to deep sadness and she became immobilized. I said to her in a very sad voice: *You are feeling so sad.* She nodded her head *yes* and two tears rolled down her cheek. Through this interaction I was able to validate Sara's feelings and at the same time allow her to view herself. Winnicott relates a vignette about a little girl who sat on his knee, bit his knuckles, cried, and played a game of throwing spatulas. He explained that while playing a game of throwing spatulas from his lap she was able to express hostile aggression and great sadness (Winnicott, 1996). Just as Winnicott's little patient was able to express her sadness through play with spatulas, Sara was able to express her sadness while playing with the baby lotion. Our play with the baby lotion touched a very deep place in Sara. Her longing to be touched was immeasurable. Her lack of physical and emotional proximity with her mother was overwhelming, causing her to feel profound sadness.

Sara's play was mechanical and joyless and possessed emptiness. However, she included me in her play and it was through her play that I was able to engage Sara on an affective level. In these early sessions she would feed a baby doll a bottle, empty out the dollhouse handing me all of the objects, or hold on to one end of a slinky and place the other end in my hand. She played in silence and I provided the narrative. *You are feeding your baby milk in her bottle,* or *You want me to hold all of the people in this dollhouse,* or *You want me to play slinky with you.*

Over the next several weeks she began to mimic me, verbally stringing together three to five words together in sentences. Her sense of her own body seemed to improve. She no longer lost her balance as easily and was better able to navigate her surroundings. She began to laugh and sustain short periods of eye contact without experiencing overwhelming anxiety. Perhaps most important, but painful, Sara began to feel deeply. She now was capable of expressing both hostile aggression and great sadness. In her play with dollhouse figures she began to act out aggressively toward the mother doll, hitting her on the head with the little girl doll, and finally stomping on the mother doll's head. She played a similar game with a stuffed squirrel family, always attacking the mother figure.

In one particular session I elicited a game of peek-a-boo that fascinated Sara and captivated her attention as she maintained deep eye contact, but this game also caused her to feel intensely sad. At first I found it extremely difficult to maintain the engagement when the therapy elicited these affects. For example, if Sara became profoundly sad in a session, I felt the need to make it all better for her, to make the bad feelings go away. I needed to be able to "hold" Sara in whatever she was feeling in the moment. It was my job to validate her feelings and show her that both she and I could survive them.

The following vignette illustrates the importance of play in the therapeutic relationship and how Sara was able to use play to communicate with me while fighting a deep depression. This vignette also illustrates the strength and meaning of attachment. This session was pivotal in our work and demonstrates how after a weekend absence, Sara felt abandoned and rejected by me.

When I went to daycare to retrieve Sara for our session I found her in a dissociated state. Daycare staff reported that she had been in this condition when her mother brought her in. She was mute, unable to walk, and did not respond when spoken to. When I picked her up to carry her to my office her body was stiff, but she offered no resistance. Once in my office she made an attempt to play by feeding a bottle to the baby doll but was unable to do this as the bottle fell from her hand. I felt at a loss and did not know what to do. I instinctively picked her up and began to pace and sing to her as if she were an infant. Slowly her body began to relax and she molded to my body and fell asleep. I sat down in my chair and, as she slept, I wondered what had happened to this little girl and how I possible could help her. We sat still for thirty minutes.

I hoped she had a high fever, for that would explain the behavior, but I knew that she was not physically ill. However my need to make her well was very powerful, so I covered her with my coat and headed back outside, across the street, and back to daycare to take her temperature. Her teacher inserted the thermometer under her arm as she slept in my arms, and of course it registered normal. As I spoke with her teachers, trying to discern if there had been some abuse of some sort, she awoke. I did not realize she was awake because she remained motionless; her teachers informed me that her eyes were open. We decided that perhaps she would want to lie on her cot, so her teacher got out her cot and I sat on the floor with Sara still motionless in my arms. She was unable to move from me. I began to talk to her very slowly and quietly, telling her how sad she was and how hard it is to feel so sad. I held her in my arms and we rocked together as I sang a lullaby. At this point the teacher came over and asked Sara if she would like to join her class in a project. Her barely audible *no* let me know she was beginning to feel safe enough to come back. I asked her if she would like to return to my office and she nodded her head *yes.*

Once back in my office I continued to sing and speak softly to her. She lay in my arms like an infant at the breast and began to explore my face. She gazed into my eyes as her fingers explored my lips. I responded to her as if she were an infant. As I continued to verbalize her sadness she slowly became able to move from me physically and began to communicate with me through her play. She handed me the toy phone. When I asked with whom I should speak, her answer was unintelligible, so I asked her if she wanted me to call her. She nodded her head *yes.* I began: *Hello Sara, you were so sad this morning that you couldn't even talk, and you couldn't even walk. But now you are beginning to feel better and we are having a safe time together.*

She returned to her continuing drama using the squirrel family. This time the mommy squirrel held the baby and did not hold the big sister. The sister became very angry and began to hit the mommy on the head. She gathered up the whole family; the mommy, baby, and sister, and threw them into my lap. I responded: *You are throwing them all at me and now I have the whole family and I can hold them in my arms.* Sara had communicated how rejected she felt by my weekend absence, and her sibling rivalry. After this conversation she came very close to me where I was sitting on the floor and she took my hair and covered my face. I said: *Where did I go? I have disappeared!* I could see her face through my hair and she became very frightened. I moved my hair away from my face and exclaimed that I was back, but that I could see how sad she had become when she thought I had gone away. She was then able to repeat this several times-both covering me up and bringing me back. As she did this she maintained eye contact. This interaction was not a happy, funny peek-a-boo game, but rather a very serious use of play.

This session lasted just under three hours. Just as we were leaving my office, Sara deliberately plucked a handful of tissues from a box near my desk. As we walked back to daycare she was able to talk with me and notice her environment. She opened her daycare door and looked back over her shoulder at me as if to give me one last look before I left her again. I watched her from the window as she rejoined her class, seated around a table to paste and paint Thanksgiving turkeys. She clutched the tissues tightly in her hand as she sat among the other children, struggling not to dissociate once again. I was shaken. I had never experienced such profound sadness in another human being.

That afternoon I met with Esther in an effort to discover some hidden abuse or mysterious illness that would cause Sara to dissociate. When I began my session with Esther I was aware of my anger toward her for not protecting her child from such intolerable pain. These feelings quickly vanished as I felt like Esther, too, was a small child crying out for connection and love. It was obvious that Esther did not abuse her daughter; she was even unaware that Sara was in this sate. Her lack of empathy for Sara was startling. Sara seemed invisible to her. For the next several sessions I helped Sara to internalize my image by providing her with Polaroid pictures and making little transitional objects during her session that she could keep with her the rest of the day. I pretended to take her picture with an imaginary camera and told her I was taking her picture to keep in my head so I could think of her. I then suggested that she take my picture to put in her head.

Continued progress

Sara continued to make progress in her ability to form attachments and in so doing began to rapidly catch up in her development. Every session I made sure a Polaroid snapshot of Sara was on my desk. Each session she would pick it up and I would ask her who it is. She always answered *Mommy*. I made a joke out of it, and while we laughed I would tell her that it is not her mommy and she would laugh but continue to tell me that it was a picture of her mom. Six months into our work together she picked up the picture and proudly said her own name. Around the same time she began to use pronouns in her speech. Sara also began to use the word *no* a lot. She seemed to feel power in that little word and it was wonderful to see her begin to gain autonomy. A few months later she became interested in toilet training and we spent session after session making clay "poop", exclaiming how glorious it was, and pretend-flushing it down the toilet. A few weeks after the interest in toilet training began, Sara began to test limits, something she had never done before. She was playing in my sink pouring water when all of a sudden I found myself soaked because she had deliberately poured a whole bottle of water on me. She thought this was hilarious and laughed a long and hard belly laugh. However, I was not pleased. I acknowledged that it made her laugh and that it seemed funny to her but that I did not want to get wet and I could not allow her to do that. We made a rule that the water stays in the sink. She immediately tried to pour water on me again. This time I was ready for her and intercepted the bottle. She took it and dumped it all over my floor. I turned off the water and she became very angry and we both tolerated her anger.

Shortly after the toilet training interest and limit testing began Sara began to "play" baby. She was aware that this play was pretend and she was in control. Over the next several weeks "Sara-baby" grew, slowly proceeding through phases of development. For example, the first several times she played the game she was a newborn infant. She made crying sounds and lay in my arms demanding that I hold her bottle and feed her and soothe her cries. This continued for several sessions. At times she could not be calmed and her cries were piercing and sounded real as if she had become that infant who could not be comforted. It was obvious that she relished her new game of pretend and told me when I picked her up at daycare for her session that we were going to play "baby". Eventually she held the bottle and fed herself. She also added eating cookies and asking to be burped while sitting in my lap.

I was taking a two-month leave and began to prepare Sara for this long absence. Sara was unable to play after this news. She disengaged from me by regressing to repetitive water play for the rest of the hour. In her next session Sara once again played "baby". She began to throw the bottle and demand that I retrieve it. Sara's play of throwing the baby bottle across the room for me to retrieve had multiple meanings. For example, this play may represent cognitive development. At this stage of development the child gains object permanence where she begins to understand that if an object is hidden it has not disappeared but is still there, just waiting to be found. It could be postulated that this play constituted a stage of cognitive development that was lagging in Sara. It is likely that Sara and her mother never engaged in a game of throw and retrieve. This play may symbolize my leaving and coming back. Sara was working through separation and loss. Sara's rage was directed at me as a real object who leaves and returns but within the transference I was Sara's mother who is often unable to meet Sara's emotional needs.

In the following sessions Sara began to crawl and retrieve her own bottle after she threw it. After this session I was away for one week. Upon my return Sara ignored me and refused to come to her session and climbed into the lap of an unknown volunteer. This was unusual behavior for Sara. She is not indiscriminate with her attention. She was telling me: *This is how it feels to be left!* However, she was also showing me that she was now capable of seeking out other adults to help her cope with difficult feelings.

Shortly after my weeklong absence, Sara, within her pretend game of "baby", began to climb to the top of my couch and fling herself off. She did this with such force that, had I not caught her, she would have hurt herself. This continued for several sessions and seeped into her other play with puppets and dollhouse figures as she showed me over and over how it feels to be dropped.

A difficult separation

During my two-month hiatus Sara's teacher provided her with postcards that I had prepared and had made a small section of wall in the classroom available for Sara to display pictures and notes from me. When I returned, at first sight of me, she burst into tears and, while sobbing, exclaimed: *I don't want to come to your office with you* as she held her arms to be picked up and carried. Her play gradually changed as she began to play baby with a doll and she became the mommy. She would spend many sessions nurturing and singing to her baby. At this point Sara rarely played the infant. However, when her mother was going through a difficult time, Sara used the "baby" game to let me know she was feeling vulnerable.

As Sara approached her fourth birthday her speech was clearer and age appropriate, she was completely toilet trained, her gait remained somewhat stiff as if she needed to be very careful to keep her balance and keep her place safe in her world, but she was able to smoothly navigate her surroundings. She communicated verbally when she was scared or angry and sought out adults for comfort. Most striking was Sara's ability to play. Her play evolved to where she made up complicated scenarios using animal figures. Using symbolic play she continued to work through feelings of being dropped and uncared for, but she also exhibited age-appropriate conflicts. With a lion family she played out Oedipal fantasies and wishes, anger toward her mother, sibling jealousies, and separation conflicts.

Connecting mother and daughter

Early on in my relationship with this family I was struck by Esther's indifference to her daughter. There were many times that Sara and I would pass Esther in the lobby as we made our way to and from daycare. In these chance meetings there would be no interaction; neither mother nor child would acknowledge the other. Every time this would occur I would give Sara a voice and supply the needed words. I would say: *Hi Mom, I am going to Miss Ann's office now. I will see you after my nap.* After this occurred several times I pushed further and said: *Hi Mom. I sure could use a morning Mommy hug,* and I would help Esther hug her daughter.

In the beginning it was difficult to get Esther to keep appointments with me. She seemed petrified, as if she expected to be scolded by me. I found myself "mother chasing". When I would see her leave the building, I would run out to catch a few words with her on the sidewalk before she quickly took off into the depths of the city streets or into the elevator as she ran from me. When she finally came for an appointment I realized that this mother longed to play as she eyed my toys and touched items with longing. So we played. We made calendars that she colored with glitter and a mommy/baby animal book that she could give to Sara for Christmas. What was most appreciated was a photo book that we made together of her little family, a book that took months to construct. As I nurtured Esther she slowly became more able to nurture Sara.

We began weekly family sessions to which Esther brought both her daughters and we sang nursery rhymes and made a nursery rhyme book that she could read to her children at home. Slowly Esther began to play with Sara. And then it happened! Sara and I met Esther on our way to my office and Sara ran to her mom shouting: *Hi Mom! I need a morning hug.* [Esther smiled and gave her a hug.] *I'm going with Ann now. See you later.* It became a regular interaction and there were several incidents where Esther initiated the "morning hug" and began to take my words as her own: *I will see you later after your nap!* There were setbacks where Esther was physically abusive and she lashed out at Sara verbally when her own life was not going well. But the improvement in the relationship was striking.

Mother stays attached

Esther and her children concluded their time at the shelter and graduated from the program. They had been given extended time in the shelter but could no longer stay. To Esther's credit she continued to bring both of her children to daycare and Sara was able to continue her therapy. Esther was helped to find housing and moved from her protected "holding" environment back out into the world where she experienced grave difficulties keeping her children safe. It was becoming increasingly apparent that Sara was being exposed to some type of sexual behavior. Her play became more driven and there was an underlying anxiety. The manifest content of the play continued to be ambiguous as she played out dramas between Mom and Dad and both daughters. These play/dramas mostly consisted of Mom and Dad kissing and the children becoming aggressive and scared. Sara ended these sessions needing physical contact. She let me know this either by regressing into her "baby" game or asking to be carried back to daycare. I felt that Sara was witnessing sexual behavior between her mother and father, who had secretly moved in with the family as it was against housing rules.

Sara's younger sister, Nancy, (two years old) began to present with disturbing symptoms. It is important to note that this child had been developing normally. She also benefited from being her mother's adored child. The daycare staff alerted me to their concerns, stating that she had stopped talking, was unhappy most of the time, and seemed to *disappear* and not hear them when they spoke to her. With my urging, Esther took Nancy to the doctor who reported that she had been sexually molested. The proper authorities were notified and Esther was terrified that her daughters would be taken from her. The sexual abuse charge was never founded and the case was closed, but the tragedy had occurred. I began to see Nancy in therapy, as no other therapist was available.

In Esther's mind I had failed her. By allowing her to leave our agency and once again venture unprotected into the world, she thought it was me who had not kept her children safe. She let me know this with intense anger toward me. It took weeks for her to begin to speak with me again. Slowly, as I built up her self-esteem and self-worth as a mother, she began to trust me again. It was my hope that Esther would join me in working with both of her daughters so they too may feel safe and protected by their mother.

Difficult problems

Sara continued working on difficult issues. She began to act out her sister's abuse and she demonstrated how unsafe she herself felt. Two weeks after I began to see Nancy in therapy, Sara refused to come with me for her session. At first I used persuasion such as quietly reminding her how important our time was together, so important it could not be missed, but that only worked once. Next I resorted to my creative powers and that helped as she pretended to be a bus driver and drive me to my office. This role-play was also useful, as she often refused to pick me up and take me to McDonald's, but at the last minute, she would leave me stranded. However, this too lost its appeal as her feelings of loss became overpowering. Eventually I resorted to picking her up and carrying her screaming all the way to my office. She would calm down as soon as we entered my office but would walk around touching things and asking: *Who did this? Who touched that?* Her play regressed to infancy, as she became the "dropped" infant. She would cry pitifully and could not be comforted. When she was not the anxious and apprehensive baby, she attempted to fling herself off the top of my couch. For weeks, this continued. As I carried her to my office from daycare her chant became *Leave me alone!* I began to hear it as: *You have left me. I am so alone.*

I addressed her feelings of loss, anger, sadness, and abandonment. I began to tell her a story about *a little girl who loved her mommy so much that she thought that her mommy would never need or desire another child. One day her mommy had a new baby and the new baby was always in mommy's arms. It made the little girl feel very sad and very angry because she wanted mommy all for herself.* Sara listened intently and it seemed to help calm her and enable her to work in her session. These were painful weeks for both of us as I attempted to help Sara work through her loss of me as the "good mother" who loves only her. She re-experienced her feelings of loss from the time when her little sister was born and her mother rejected her even more forcefully than when she was an infant. The following vignette is from Sara's last session before an unexpected and abrupt break in our work. In retrospect it is apparent that Sara was fearful that she was about to lose me.

As soon as I entered her classroom, she began to wail and moan. Sara grabbed hold of the child nearest to her and begged him to protect her from me. He came to her aid and blocked me with his body as she hung onto his back. Sara's teacher was visibly upset as I explained to the little boy that I was not going to hurt Sara, but that it was important for her to have her special time with me. He understood this, as he too has a "special time" with a beloved therapist. As I carried Sara kicking and screaming, *Leave me alone,* she began to try to hit me in the face. I retold her the "little girl story" that had come to be known as just "the story". As usual she was calmed by the story but she remained angry. She picked up the two old phones, handed one to me, and called me. *Ring ring!* I answered and she said: *Did you take Nancy?* I said: *You are thinking about how I take your sister and it makes you feel very angry with me and so very sad because you want me all for yourself.* Sara slammed the phone down in its cradle. She called me several times each time I answered she slammed down the phone and refused to speak. This play caused her to experience overwhelming anxiety, and she did something that she had not done for almost two years: she began to open and slam my desk drawer. The large bang caused her to laugh hysterically. I said: *Remember when you were little, so little you wore diapers and you would come here and when you felt bad feelings inside you would bang this drawer? I think you are feeling that now.* Sara smiled. She then began a game of leaving me behind. She enacted this with little Fisher Price figures: she was the mom who came to pick me, the child, up and before I could get into the car she would race off. It was torture. Her message was evident when she picked up the little house, all the little people, and their car and threw it all into my garbage. She sat back and began to cry like an infant. I asked her if she wanted to play baby and held out my arms to her. She shook her head *yes* and climbed into my arms. I fed her cookies and a bottle and sang her a special lullaby that was all about how she was feeling. She accepted this nurturing and quickly settled down and was once again able to play. It was time to end the session so I suggested that the house and all the people did not always feel so bad and that maybe we could rescue them from the garbage. She agreed to this and locked up all the people safely inside the house. However, before locking it all up, she attempted to put her own head into the little house. I said: *You just want to be locked up all safe with me.* She began a game of *knock, knock,* a word game she always enjoyed, but this time when it was my turn and I said *It's Miss Ann,* she corrected me and said: *No, you are Miss Ann Williams!* She insisted that her last name was mine.

Discussion

Sara quickly learned that her world was a cold and unfriendly, and she withdrew to a safer place. Her pain must have reached intolerable limits. Fraiberg suggests that when the infant withdraws into herself it is a primitive defense, which serves to obliterate the intolerable pain (Fraiberg, 1982). Slade states that when a mother grossly misinterprets, misreads, or ignores her child's needs the child develops inadequate methods of communicating those needs to the parent (Slade, 1998). Winnicott tells us that when an infant is left too long without human contact the child's experience can only be described by "such words as: going to pieces; falling for ever; dying and dying and dying" (Winnicott, 1987, p. 86). When Sara became distressed she just went to sleep. Bowlby suggests that when children experience neglect they form numerous and intrinsically conflicting representations of the same reality (Bowlby, 1988). As Sara grew, her primitive defenses helped her to keep unwanted feelings from her consciousness. Sara dissociated from her feelings.

Fraiberg, Adelson, and Shapiro, in their famous article "Ghosts in the Nursery", ask the question "Why doesn't this mother hear her baby's cries?" (Fraiberg, Adelson, & Shapiro, 1975, p. 344). We saw that Sara had taken on her mother's affective life. Esther's sadness was mirrored in Sara's whole being. In a healthy relationship between mother and infant the mother reflects back to her infant, the infant's affect. Thus, when the child gazes into her mother's face she sees herself (Winnicott, 1987; Beebe, Lachmann, & Jaffe, 1997). Esther was unable to mirror Sara's own feeling states; instead Sara looked into her mother's face and what was reflected back was a misrepresentation of her emerging self.

She took on as her core representation of herself her mother's "distorted and barren picture of the child" (Fonagy & Target, 1998, p. 95). Sara's early attempts to engage her mother had failed, so she found a "way-of-being-with-mother" (Stern, 1995, p. 101) by identifying and mirroring her mother's depression. Esther's own history of rejection, neglect, and abandonment was now being reenacted with her daughter. Sara's emotional needs were too threatening for Esther to bear. Her own defense was to deny similar feelings pertaining to her own early relationships. Sara's yearning to be held and loved, coupled with her fears and anger, caused Esther to feel and remember her own intolerable memories (Slade, 1998). Esther's own infant cries were probably rarely comforted. Her pain needed to be acknowledged and her story needed to be told and witnessed. "When this mother's own cries are heard, she will hear her child's cries" (Fraiberg, Adelson, & Shapiro, 1975, p. 395). But meanwhile Sara was suffering and could not wait for her mother, so treatment began.

Sara and I created a "transitional space" (Winnicott, 1971), and I accepted her stipulations of engagement. Through use of attunement, mirroring, and empathy, Sara slowly began to engage. The therapy provided a holding function wherein Sara was able to feel safe and contained and experienced pleasure. However she was in control as I respected her necessary defenses against painful affects (King, 1993). My office became a safe environment where she could regress to infancy, act out in rage against her mother, safely test limits, and enact many other emotions that would be too dangerous for her mother or other adults in her life to tolerate.

Because Sara had endured profound neglect I imagine that she had few experiences of physical comfort and affection. The social environment of this family was intrusive and fragmented. Esther's own inner life must have been one of chaos. She was unable to respond to her infant's signals; perhaps she ignored them or misread them. Her own profound depression and life circumstances caused her to be preoccupied and unavailable to Sara. One only had to spend a few minutes with this mother to understand that she was hungry and starving in her own way. Esther was unable to provide her infant daughter with attunement that is necessary for secure attachment (Greenspan, 1990; Hughes, 1997; Karen, 1998).

In the normal mother/infant relationship affect regulation occurs through attunement, mirroring, and empathy. In the beginning of our work together, whenever Sara expressed an emotion I mirrored it for her. In this way she had the opportunity to learn to regulate and integrate her feeling states so that she could begin to develop a sense of herself as different from others. It is through this mechanism that the core origin of self begins to emerge (Shore, 1994). In a healthy relationship the mirroring that occurs between a mother and child is not just a mere reflection of behavior but rather is more like a "magical mirror" (Coates, 1998, p. 122). The mother reflects back to her infant her potential, thus creating the space for the infant to experience herself. Coates states "the mother's ability to see the potential in the infant is what allows the infant to find if for himself or herself, in the face of the mother" (Coates, 1998, p. 122). It is this type of mirroring that I attempted to achieve with Sara.

If all goes well for an infant and an affective, pleasurable relationship has been formed, "then with growing maturational abilities the infant develops complex patterns of communication in the context of this primary relationship" (Greenspan, 1990, p. 154). Sara had learned that her attempts to communicate elicited very little or no response. Therefore her sensory and motor skills, so vital to engagement, did not develop. Because of this disruption in the attachment process, Sara did not learn "to appreciate causal relationships between people and to experience compassionate and intimate feelings" (Greenspan, 1990, p. 154). Early in my work with Sara she withdrew from my touch and her "play" was mechanical and repetitive. She had learned that little value was placed on communication, and thus she did not have the ability to "facilitate the recognition and expression of thoughts and ideas" (Hughes, 1997, p. 25).

When life is good and things go well, the human relationship grows as the infant develops. As the mother provides protection, comfort, and regularity, an emotional attachment is formed. In this way the parent facilitates her baby's developmental growth (Greenspan, 1990). My job with Sara was to form a connected relationship. I did this by deeply engaging her on an affective level. Sara responded and quickly began to catch-up in her development.

The day after Sara dissociated I questioned that perhaps Sara may have been physically ill, even autistic. Upon reflection I realized Sara had formed an attachment to me and my absence, just over a weekend, struck a deep, primitive wound in her. It became unbearable for her to feel loss and she probably experienced an anaclitic depression.

In our early weeks of work together I played with Sara as a mother plays with her infant. She experienced what it is to be played with and to be playful. My absence brought on feelings of annihilation. Sara may have lost "all vestige of hope of the renewal of contacts" (Winnicott, 1987, p. 86). She had not reached object constancy in her development and was unable to internalize my image. When we were apart she experienced it as desertion. I incorporated in our play the use of a Polaroid camera. Photographs, along with other homemade transitional objects, became essential in our work.

When I took Sara's younger sister as a patient I had let Sara down and hurt her terribly. Sara was both furious with me and fearful that she had lost me. On another level Sara was able to bring into her therapy the experience of losing what little attention and love she received from her mother when her sibling was born. Esther was open about her bias toward Nancy. Nancy was the preferred and loved child while Sara was pushed further back in her mother's mind and continued to experience rejection. Esther often expressed the idea that Sara embarrassed her and openly displayed disgust toward her daughter.

As noted in the clinical material, Sara regressed back to infancy where she could not be comforted. Her cries were those of a tiny infant screaming in anguish. When she attempted to fling herself from the top of my couch, it could be interpreted as falling forever because she felt unloved and worthless. When a child feels this, "it leaves the child alone with the devastating thought that it is better not to be alive than not being loved" (Lussier, 1999, p. 155).

Winnicott speaks of "the gradual failure that has to be experienced by the child when the parents are not available" (Winnicott, 1987, p. 21). Perhaps Sara's ego was not yet strong enough to tolerate my *realness* and she could not permit frustration. She had not had sufficient experiences of omnipotence and had yet to develop a sense of self. Winnicott reminds us that the growing sense of self through time is reinforced by the mother's empathic responses. It is this mother/infant dance that strengthens the child's sense of her own omnipotence (Winnicott, 1978). My reactions were felt by Sara as being insensitive to her ego needs, and this led to her feeling disintegration, withdrawal, and a feeling of annihilation.

As difficult as these months were it was an opportunity for me to help Sara realize that no matter how hard she tried to destroy me I would survive and be there for her. Her re-experiencing the loss of her mother's love when her little sister was born also gave me the opportunity to help Sara learn new and more adaptive ways of coping.

Fonagy argues that a major role of the therapist is to help children learn to think reflectively or to be able to mentalize. I feel I did this as I assisted Sara in labeling and thus understanding her emotional states. This is seen very early on in our work when Sara became extremely sad when I rubbed lotion on her arm. By helping her to view herself as feeling sadness she began "to understand both the conscious and the unconscious relationships between [her] behavior and internal states" (Fonagy & Target, 1998, p. 105). Sara's emotions and affects changed quickly within a session and by staying with her in the moment, I taught her how others see and know her. She took on my perceptions of her inner states as her own self-perceptions and this facilitated the emergence of her core self (Fonagy & Target, 1998; Stern, 1985). Through our therapeutic relationship, Sara found a way of thinking about and coping with her feelings. Just as she learned as a newborn that the only way to be with her mother was to take on her depressive and flat affective qualities, she now learned a *new way of being* with another person. She was able to take her *new way of being* and offer it to her mother. Luckily, Esther responded, due in part to feeling nurtured and held by me, and Sara and Esther began to relate in a healthier, growth-promoting fashion.

Giving Sara words: *Hi Mom, I need a morning hug!* and helping Esther to see and hear her child gradually over the months transformed Esther's understanding of her daughter. She began to be able to see Sara as a separate individual. Esther's projections and distortions became fewer, which was an essential contribution to Sara's growth (Slade, 1998). On Sara's end of the interaction, she had learned to "avoid placing an attachment demand upon a parent who would not tolerate it and who might react by creating greater distance between them" (Stern, 1995, p. 106). Over time and with many repetitions, Esther became more of a secure base for her child as Sara became able to verbally ask her mother for a "morning hug" and Esther responded with genuine joy.

Conclusion

It has been documented that securely attached children are more capable of making use of symbolic play. Therapists often use symbolic play as a means of assessing the child's ability to be self-reflective (Karen, 1998;

Fonagy & Target, 1998). As described, Sara lived her first two years on the street, and her next three years in a homeless shelter. Sara's mother had severe cognitive limitations, which made it difficult for her to view her child as a separate person with a mind of her own. As Sara formed an attachment to me and then was able to transfer what she learned from our relationship to her relationship with her mother her play changed. Sara gradually was able to play symbolically, as evidenced in her play with animal families and in her "baby" game. Sara had entered the world of imagination and make-believe and her life became much more enjoyable and bearable.

When Sara entered therapy she had limited capacity to play. Her play was stilted, mechanical, repetitive, and joyless. Her affect was constricted and she had few resources for coping. Her development had been severely compromised. As our relationship developed, I helped her to imagine and create through the use of both words and play, and she began to symbolize. In her play she was gradually able to express profound sadness and tremendous rage. As I labeled her affects they were given meaning and brought into understanding. This enabled Sara to begin to understand her world, including both inner fantasies and reality. As she began to make meaning of her own inner world she also developed the ability to understand and relate to others. Sara began to experience herself as "known" and therefore as a separate individual with a sense of self. Sara's body began to regulate, as her toilet training illustrated, and her affective expression changed. Her dejection and joyless behavior gave way to a delightful sense of humor and an enjoyment of the world. What was most helpful in Sara's growth was Esther's ability to begin to imagine her child's experience. As successful as I was in meeting Sara's inner mental state, it was Esther's own growth and healing that was most beneficial. Crucial to Sara's growth was the act of giving voice through symbolic play to Sara's inner world. As Sara felt safe enough to form an attachment she began to learn to think reflectively and as a result she has attained a more differentiated and integrated sense of self (Mahler et al., 1975). Sara's ability to form attachments and make meaning of her inner thoughts and feelings had given her a new-found resiliency that enabled her to seek out new attachment figures. Most importantly, Sara was able to make contact with her mother at a time when Esther was unable to reach out to her.

Had Sara not entered intensive analytic treatment when she did it is possible that she would have been diagnosed as severely mentally retarded and eventually been institutionalized. Sara now has a chance for a life where she will become a functional member of society. Sara's story illustrates the need for combined attachment work to be done with the mother and her children. The tragedy that befell this family demonstrates, albeit painfully, the need for housing for cognitively limited women who wish to keep their families safe and together.

CHAPTER FOUR

The hopeless child

eorgie was adopted from an Asian country at eight months of age by two gay men, Herb and Tony. There are few details of his prenatal and birth history although it is known that he had low Apgar scores. It is also known that he was born in the same hospital that became his home for his first eight months of life. Georgie was left flat on his back in a crib with minimal stimulation for this whole period of his life. I viewed videos taken at three months, six months, and eight months. It was striking and quite disturbing to watch him deteriorate over the course of his first eight months. In the first video he looked to be a newborn, at six months he seemed about two months old, and at eight months he looked disturbed, almost psychotic, not unlike the infants that Renee Spitz first introduced us to in his landmark film on hospital-ized infants. In this last video, and when Herb traveled across the world to retrieve him, Georgie lay on his back with a blank wide eyed stare with his palms up extended out in front. Herb was distraught upon meeting his new son and felt if he did not go through with the adoption that Georgie would surely die. Herb described this time as extremely stressful, as diapers were not used and Georgie was often covered in his own excrement. Herb noticed almost immediately that Georgie did not seem to respond to sound. It was determined that Georgie had complete hearing loss. Once in the United States, tests determined that there was no physiologically damage. His deafness was caused by undiagnosed ear infections and understimulation. Within a few months his hearing was restored to normal.

Georgie responded to physical affection and developed an engaging smile. His gross motor development played a quick catch-up and he was walking by thirteen months. Language development was delayed. His fathers quickly put several supports into place. He had occupational and speech therapy, had tubes placed in his ears, underwent multiple surgeries for a left strabismus, and had his adenoids removed. Georgie continued to have weak jaw muscles, which resulted in intermittent drooling. He also had a tendency to be aggressive with other children, especially his younger brother, John. John was adopted from a different country just one year after Georgie's adoption. John also experienced his first nine months of life in an institution but one where he was the only baby. To his advantage he was given a lot of attention by a primary caretaker and seemed to develop normally. John is more advanced than Georgie in many areas.

Georgie's presenting problems

Georgie was afraid of new experiences and had difficulties changing from one activity to the next. He was often socially inappropriate, intruding into another's physical space. In his pre-school class, he urinated on the floor, and clogged up toilets and sinks, and hid behind the toilet. Georgie became extremely upset when punished and would, at times, punch himself in the head. He often disregarded warnings from his father, running into the street or in front of cars in parking lots. All of these behaviors and symptoms brought five-year-old Georgie to my office where, after a short evaluation period, his analysis began.

The beginning of his analysis

At our first meeting I was struck by five-year-old Georgie's skinny awkward appearance. It was easy to see where other children might find him "different" as his ears stuck out and his eyes were wide apart with a large forehead. Most striking was his non-relatedness. He non-discriminately hugged me and came easily with me up the stairs to my playroom. His parting from his father was remarkable as there were no goodbyes by either of them and no acknowledgement upon reunion. He was well informed by his fathers as to who I was and why he was coming. He picked up the basketball and as he adeptly made baskets he told me that he knew all about me and wondered if *babies with worries* came to see me. In this first session he also showed me through doll-house play, angry interactions between his fathers, and his own conflicted feelings concerning his own aggression toward his father.

For weeks Georgie's anxiety caused him to quickly stop his play and move from activity to activity as feelings and fantasies became intolerable. During these weeks he did not include me in his play, was unable to sustain eye contact and left without a goodbye. My countertransference was impressive as I was left to feel as if I did not matter or perhaps did not even really exist in his world. Georgie gradually engaged, but only through aggression. His threw balls at me hard as he aimed for my head or hit me hard on the leg.

Georgie began to play a game using magnetic marbles where we were people and our bodies kept coming apart. At the end of this game he connected his body to mine and announced that we were now "combined!" Within this game of connecting and coming apart, Georgie demonstrated his difficulties in relating and his feelings about the fragility of his own body. Our connection was precarious, easily broken as the magnetic marbles simply fell apart and recombined. There was a hopeless feeling in these interactions.

Georgie began to talk about my upcoming vacation, reacting to the impending separation, telling me that he did not want me to go away. He used the sand and made me a house and buried me in the sand, house and all.

A: *Now I'm stuck in my house and can't go on my vacation.*
G: *It's not you. It's a nobody and when you put sand on a nobody they melt into a nothing.*
A: *That seems sad. First I am a nobody and then you turn me into a nothing.*

In this play he made it impossible for me to leave. I speculate that this separation brought on early feelings of profound loss and hopelessness. He was worried about losing me. If he attached to me he risked experiencing devastating loss upon separation and a return of a devastating feeling of hopelessness resulting in annihilation anxiety. The worst feeling of all is to feel as if you are a *nobody*. Georgie turned it around and made me feel what it is like to be a *nothing*. A heaviness filled the room and embraced us both. I felt hopeless at that moment.

As our work continued and I interpreted his rage in the transference, his aggressive behavior in the play directed toward me ended. I pointed out to him that on some days he could look at me and our eyes really saw each other and that on other days, feelings inside of him seemed to be uncomfortable and at these times his eyes could not look into mine. He gazed deeply into my eyes and replied:

G: *Sometimes I can look at you and sometimes I just can't! I tricked Pa. I told him I didn't want to come here but I really did!* [He repeats this statement several times obviously distressed]
A: *Maybe part of you wanted to come here so we could work on your worries and maybe part of you didn't want to come here all at the same time.*
G: *Yes! That's it. I wanted to and didn't want to all at the same time.*

Looking and not looking was an important concept that caused Georgie distress. He could not allow himself to look because if he looked he would care. By not looking he protected himself and me. In addition, he was preserving his relationship with his father, knowing, on some level, that Herb was not able to tolerate the inclusion of a third person, especially a mother-figure. The ability to make use of the triadic relationship was threatening and completely absent. I found myself feeling constantly on edge around Herb. I too felt that relatedness and attachment in this family was dangerous. I began to fear that Herb would end treatment precipitously.

Less then a year into our work, in reaction to my vacation and Georgie's worries about losing me, "Mother" material entered his analysis. His analysis provided him the opportunity to begin to consider his lost mother. A female family friend had died and Georgie was friendly with the surviving child. He told me he was very sad because this little boy never had a daddy and now he also had no mother. He added that he had a Dad and a Pa and his family is a boy family. There is no mother. He attempted to enter into pretend play but clearly had many thoughts that he needed to verbalize.

G: *I was just wondering and I don't know how a person can get sick and die.*

A: *You are worried about that. It is upsetting and very worrisome that a Mommy can just get sick and die, leaving her son with no mommy and no daddy.*

G: *I had a mommy one time a long time ago and my mommy died. She died before I was alive.*

A: *You don't remember your mommy.*

G: *I have a Dad and a Pa.*

For weeks his play was about magic potions that kept mommies and boys alive forever, until one morning when he came in and stated that he was never inside a mommy's tummy, that his Dad bought him from another country. Weeks later he told me he was never born, but rather was a "bug that evolved into a boy". This material demonstrated that Georgie had multiple fantasies about his origin and what happened to his mother. I expressed my concern to his fathers about Georgie's confusion over his birth story. His parents were waiting for him to ask about his mother before offering any information. It is important to note that this young family had little outside emotional support. Tony's experience with his own father was tumultuous. His father was an alcoholic who was physically and verbally abusive. Tony's homosexuality had never been accepted by either of his parents and he remained estranged from them. Herb's father died after a prolonged chronic illness when Herb was a young boy. Herb's mother suffered from mental illness leaving Herb to become her caretaker from as young as he could remember. Thus neither father had worked through their own unresolved childhood traumas. Both Herb and Tony had poor attachment histories, tinged with rage over separations. I wondered to myself why Herb adopted Georgie. He had told me that if he left him in that hospital he would have surely died. I speculate there were other motivations as well. Perhaps Herb fantasized that Georgie would provide the love and relatedness he never had. Perhaps his vision was that Georgie would be totally attached to him (and only him) forever.

I suggested that they might want to consider speaking with both boys about their adoptions. Georgie obviously knew on some level that he was adopted, but his story had remained a secret and unspeakable. A few days later Herb left me a message that the talk had taken place. Georgie comes into his next session in obvious distress:

G: *I don't want to talk about it!*

A: *It is hard to talk about your Mom.*

G: *I give up! I give up!* [exasperated and distressed]
A: *So many confusing feelings.*
G: *Yes lots of feelings.*
A: *So many different feelings all at the same time all mixed up.*
G: *She gave me away!* [He picks up a ball and throws it at my face]

He was furious with his mother for giving him away and also enraged that I had left him and had taken a vacation. He had to kill off the mother (and fathers) as he played that we were two orphaned boys who were adopted by two fathers, but our fathers were killed, leaving us all alone in the world once again.

The second year of analysis

As his analysis proceeded into the second year, the mother transference deepened. In the play, sometimes we were husband and wife as Georgie became charmingly seductive and flirtatious. This play would shift and he would make me Pa and we would become two fathers who adopted many, many boys. For weeks we played out this same scenario until one day he asked me to walk him to my waiting room and for the first time he turned to me, made eye contact and, with a seductive smile, said goodbye. Georgie's provocative performance gave me an uneasy feeling. I knew Herb would experience this interaction as extremely threatening. Herb continued to ignore me at the beginning and end of sessions and reunions of father and son continued to be silent and distant. As the analysis moved forward it became increasingly clear to me that both Georgie and his father were unable to tolerate what felt like me intruding into the dyad. Georgie needed the triadic relatedness (even though he was unable to tolerate it) and attempted to provide it, but did so in a destructive provocative manner. Herb was incapable of allowing a third person in; he could not share his son.

Herb's inability to enter into a triadic relationship was unmistakably demonstrated as the school year ended and Georgie began summer camp. One week into the new summer schedule Herb announced that this would be Georgie's last session. He refused to come in to discuss his decision and I was left with my jaw hanging open as Georgie waited for me in my playroom. I was successful in conveying my alarm over abruptly ending treatment and Herb consented to one session per week.

I was in a difficult position as Herb refused to speak with me. I was never given the opportunity to help Herb gain some understanding of what was transpiring in his son's treatment. All I could do was wait. In six weeks' time I received a call from Herb, who was clearly distressed. I met with both fathers, and they told me how regressed Georgie had become, biting and spitting at other children. They asked me to take him back into analysis. Herb had taken Georgie away from his analysis and of course from me, but Georgie was ingeniously able to get his treatment back. I feel this speaks to evidence of his developing ego strength of this now seven-year-old little boy. He did not collapse into his feces (like in his infancy) but instead figured out a way to get his father to understand that he needed his analysis. Georgie had hope.

Herb became increasingly upset and disarmed by Georgie's close relationship with me. He began to use threats of not seeing me to get Georgie to behave and he was increasingly hostile toward me, stating that there have been no improvements; in fact he was worse and that analysis is not his treatment of choice. Herb felt I was stealing away his child, taking all the good while he was left with only the bad. No amount of parent education alleviated his intense negative transference toward me. During this period of time Georgie was overwhelmed with the worry of losing me and demonstrated this by bringing his symptoms into the treatment. He urinated all over my bathroom, filled my toilet with a whole roll of toilet paper after defecating, ripped the cup holder off the wall, punched himself in the face and banged his head on the floor. After much contemplation it was decided that Herb would join us in session once per week. Georgie was extremely displeased with this arrangement claiming that Dad was intruding on his private time.

Triadic treatment

I was quite anxious about bringing Herb into the treatment. I was concerned that Herb might feel criticized by me. I somehow wanted to help Herb and Georgie view their conflicts without causing Herb to feel incompetent or a failure as a father. Herb and Georgie's first joint session was filled with tension. Herb was immediately intrusive into Georgie's play, asking questions that demanded a correct answer. Georgie regressed to his very first interaction in the playroom and began to play basketball. Herb commented on all correctly thrown balls. Finally Georgie told his dad that he did not wish to be watched.

G: *Don't look at me!*
D: *Are you worried I will judge you? I love you. Does it feel like I don't love you?*

Georgie becomes very silly and falls to the floor.

A: *Um Georgie has become very silly. I'm wondering if something feels uncomfortable? Dad, what do you think about these silly feelings Georgie is having right now.* [Georgie hides]
D: *I see he is hiding now* [he jumps out of his hiding place with a loud Boo!]
A: *I'm thinking that maybe you don't want Dad to look at you and you do want Dad to look at you all at the same time. Something got uncomfortable and you told Dad not to look, then the silly feelings came, then the hiding feelings. But you jumped up with a loud Boo and a big smile. I think you want Dad to look and not look.*

Georgie agrees and puts his head down, visibly upset and begging his father to leave the room.

G: *I don't want you here. It feels very bad.*
D: *But Georgie I want to be part of your life. I want to know what you do in here.*
G: *It doesn't mean you aren't part of my life if you don't come in here. I don't want you here. Please leave.*

Herb refused to leave so Georgie ran out of the playroom and out of my waiting room. Herb ran after and carried him back, allowing him to come alone with me, but he was angry. Once upstairs and safe in the playroom Georgie was quite agitated and explained that his dad *is the busiest man in the world and does not know how to play.* I wondered if we could work together to help Dad learn how to play. He gathered up "Fragile", a figure that represented himself, and cupping it in his hand tenderly, he carried it down to the waiting room and explained to his father why Fragile had to be handled with care. Dad came back into the playroom where Georgie destroyed Fragile, and he and Georgie, head-to-head, gently and carefully put him back together. Another game, one that Herb directs, commences, and the attempt to direct causes Georgie to once again banish his father to the waiting room. This time Herb went seemingly feeling relieved. Later that afternoon I processed the session with Herb who was moved by my interpretation of Fragile. Herb opened up and spoke at length about his own painful childhood experiences and spoke of his identification with his young son.

The joint sessions continued on a weekly basis and a transformation occurred; Georgie went running into his father's arms at the end of his session. In addition Georgie began bringing Herb into every session, but at the very end. A ritual began where he would hide, I would call Herb up from the waiting room and state in a concerned voice that Georgie had gone missing and the only one he wanted to find him was his Dad. Herb would find him and carry him away (however, Herb's hide-and-seek skills were very lacking!). Georgie would wave to me as he molded to his father's body and smiled blissfully. This ritual continued for several months. At this point in the analysis I wondered if Georgie had made his own little Oedipal family? Had I become the mother, not only in the transference, but also in fantasy? Was I the biological parent in disguise?

I was aware that Georgie's intense transference toward me, and his ever-present wish that I could be his mother, put him in a terrible dilemma. Herb made it clear that I was the enemy. Georgie found himself in a horrific conflict: if he loved me he was betraying his father and would have to face his father's rage and threaded abandonment. It is my belief that Georgie's intense mother transference and my inability to help Herb tolerate this process led to the forced termination of Georgie's analysis.

Nine months before last session

The following session took place nine months before termination. I had broken my back during my summer vacation and was wearing a body brace. In this particular session I had been in the brace for almost two months when Georgie brought it up. During this time, I was unable to sit on the floor and Georgie was extremely accommodating bringing his play scenarios to my chair so I would not have to move about.

I waited at the top of the stairs (it was difficult for me to navigate the stairs with my broken back) as Georgie climbed up to meet me. He gives my brace a long look and says:

G: *How much longer do you have to wear that?*
A: *About two more weeks. I can see that you are thinking about my brace and*
     my injury.
G: *I was thinking that you look like a spider with white legs.*

A: *Umm. Sounds scary.*

G: *It could be scary but I know it's a cast and I was just wondering how much longer? Will you be able to bend down and move like this* [shows me] *when you take it off?*

A: *You're wondering if I will be different or if I will be my old self.* [Georgie demonstrates how I look]

G: *It keeps you looking like this* [shows me]

A: *It keeps my back very straight.*

G: *Are your muscles okay?*

A: *I'm wondering if you have worries about my body being okay?*

G: *Maybe your muscles are weak. Will it take a long time to make them strong again?*

A: *I think I will have to do my exercises to make them strong again. You are having lots of thoughts and feelings about me today.*

G: *Will you be glad to get the spider brace off?*

A: *Yes, Georgie, I will be very glad but I am trying to be patient. Sometimes it is difficult to be patient when you have to do something that you don't like very much.*

G: *What shall we do today?* [walks around the playroom for a few seconds] *Oh I know just what to do!*

He picks a small metal car for each of us to be. They are our characters.

G: *We are friends but we live apart.*

His car zooms past my head several times.

G: *You wonder what and who I am.*

A: *I wonder what that was that just flashed before my eyes?*

G: *This is a portal between our houses. Hi I'm your new neighbor come through the portal. Come live with me in my house. I change my mind. You better live over there in your own house.*

A: *Well it seems that we can live in our separate houses but stay connected by this portal that you built for us.*

G: *I built you something else.* [He makes a contraption] *This is a special contraption that teaches you how to fall without getting hurt.*

A: *This new contraption will keep me safe in case I fall.*

G: *My house is very fancy. I am the richest boy in the whole world. My name is even Mr. Rich. That is how rich I am. I was named for my money.*

A: *How is it that you are just a boy and yet you live alone?*

G: *That is a very long story. My father sent checks of lots of money. He paid to have somebody take care of me. I send the money back. Here is a robot for you and one for me. They take care of us.*

A: *These robots can feed us but they don't have feelings. I don't think they can love us.*

G: *Don't worry you will get your love from me. Now we discover that we are lost brothers. We were born together in a large nursery. Look at our pictures. There are pictures of us as babies together.* [He throws balls down on us] *These balls fell, on the nursery and blew you away when you were just a baby. I'm in jail* [He makes a jail putting in furniture from the doll house making it a very nice place] *Let's go on adventures in this jail truck.*

A: *Where shall we go?*

G: *The best places in all of the United States but we have to leave it. This is an underground hidden place. No one can see us here or hear us or even think about us.*

He covers up the jail truck and leaves the playroom to use the bathroom. His session is over and as he leaves he explains that today he will have a *great day!*

At this point I felt things were going better with Herb. He was calling more, and seemed to be more receptive to parent education. I held guarded optimism that our work would continue for some time to come.

Session: the beginning of the end (a week had passed since our last session)

Herb had a car-pooling problem on this day because Tony was out of town. Herb asked me to see Georgie an hour later then usual. I had explained to Herb that I had to run out of my office immediately after the session but I could see him at a later time.

Georgie runs in ten minutes early, breathless. *I came as fast as I could. I know you have to leave.* He wondered around the playroom a bit disorganized trying to remember what we played in his last session. I spoke with him about missing a whole week together and being afraid he would even miss me today ... that I might have to leave. Georgie retrieved his box of transformers and chose Fragile (he named this toy three years ago, early in his analysis). *My body is fragile because my arm is broken.* I spoke about broken bones and feeling fragile and how a boy may worry about his body. He agreed that broken bones are worrisome but added that his cast kept him nice and warm in this cold weather. In the plays he is a transformer with a human heart. I am also a transformer and we are friends. *I can feel a beat in my heart. I don't hear the beep I feel it. The beep tells me I have a long lost brother somewhere.* He explained that he and his brothers had all the same parts and had good times together but the brothers got lost. He got a cup and sucked out all the bad memories and leaves only the good memories. *Beeps are happening, beeps are happening. That means there are more lost brothers. Fred, Roscoe, Jety. I have a lost mother who was three parts transformer and one part heart. My father was the same.*

Georgie brings all his dead relatives back to life except his mother whom he is unable to revive. Everyone falls and dies once again. In a frenzy he brings them back to life again. I am attacked because I am a girl and girls are very bad. *All boys hate girls.* He ends the game abruptly. I point out that something had occurred when he attacked me and told me that all boys hate girls and he had to stop the game. *No, we will take it up again tomorrow. Let's do something else.*

He got us each a car and a marble and we move in together in the dollhouse. It is time to end. *We aren't going to pick this up tomorrow after all. Please clean it up after I leave.*

Herb was waiting for me at my car and informed me that Georgie would not make the rest of his sessions this week.

Session: three weeks later

In this session, old material from his earliest days in his analysis comes back. He comes in all bedraggled from the rain complaining about his wet hair and the cold. He sits in front of the space heater drying his hair. We are each a marble. Georgie wants us to live separately in different houses. He kidnaps my grandfather and me and kills us. *Don't worry, I'm dead also.* I wonder what it feels like to be dead. *No feelings that's what its like no feelings at all.* He becomes distressed, kicks over our houses, and ends the game. I comment that the "dead" feelings came and he had to stop our game. He begins a new game. In this drama we are both cars. *I am the richest boy in the whole world because I took my grandfather's money. My grandfather was a bear. Isn't it funny that my grandfather is a bear? How in the world did I get to be a car?* [Yes that really is very curious. How is it that you are a car when your grandfather was a bear?] *Well, my mother is a dog and my father too and my other father is a dog and my other mother is also a dog.* [So you have a grandfather who is a bear and two mothers and two fathers who are dogs. Tell me how did you end up with two mothers?] *My fathers each got married and I got two mothers! Now I have to get rid of you. I can't take you all the time. Once a month you have to go live somewhere else.* He takes me to the dollhouse and he destroys the dollhouse dumping all of the furniture out onto the floor. *An evil wind came and did this destroying. Can I tell you something for real? I'm getting bad feelings. I need to stop this game before it gets to a bad point.* [Something feels very bad, maybe even dangerous. Can you tell me more about the feelings?]

The game of speedy

He begins a ball game, he makes many rules, and we play quietly by his rules. I tell him that this game seems to help him to control the bad feelings. *Yes it does. Let's play Speedy!* Speedy is a character from early in his treatment. He is a little ball named Speedy who is the fastest boy in the world and I am his proud mom.

In this drama he brings in a father. Speedy does wonderful things for his father. He gets him a great job and lots of money. Everyone is proud of him because he finished all the years of school in less then a second. Georgie wraps Speedy up in a blanket and puts him to bed next to his mom. I recap the session pointing out all of the difficult, dangerous feelings and how he was able to feel better and we ended up in a loving game.

A few weeks later he tells me that his father no longer has enough money for heat in the house so he may have to stop coming to see me. He is distressed. Right after this Herb intrudes himself into Georgie's sessions almost every day. These are difficult interactions where Herb is often mean and demanding of his son. Georgie often runs out of the room. There was one extremely terrible session where Georgie asked for his private time and his father screamed at him "You can have your precious private time. I'm leaving!" and storms out of the office. Georgie mournfully sobs. I felt that I was in a most difficult situation. Neither Georgie nor his father could entertain being in a triadic relationship. When Georgie begged for his "private time", Herb became enraged and threatened abandonment and total rejection.

The end

Herb called to let me know he had found another therapist for nine-year-old Georgie. I asked him to give us some time to say goodbye. Herb seemed to understand this but was unable to follow through and ended the treatment abruptly two weeks after our phone call.

This is hard for me. I will miss you. Maybe I won't like my new therapy. I only go see him once a week. Daddy doesn't want me to come here. Maybe I can come back here. Maybe when I am grown I can come back.

He made up a game where I am a toilet and he treats me very badly. The game ends where I am left all alone destroyed.

For the last ten days of his analysis, Georgie and I made two houses out of Lego. He used every Lego piece. He connected our houses and he put the mom figure inside and blocked up all the windows. On a Friday his father told me the following Monday would be the last session.

Georgie spent his last session taking apart our co-created Lego house. It took almost the whole forty-five minutes to dismantle it. *I can't leave this, it has to come apart. I will always remember you.* I felt very sad to see Georgie leave for the last time.

Discussion

Renee Spitz shocked the medical community with his video proof of "hopeless" children. The term anaclitic depression was first formulated by Spitz (1946). Infants after six months of age who experienced prolonged separations from their primary caretaker developed symptoms of weeping, apathy, inactivity, withdrawal, sleep problems, weight loss, and developmental regressions, which he gave this label. In addition, feelings of loneliness, helplessness, and fear of abandonment are now understood to be a part of the syndrome. If adequate mothering is re-established within a reasonable time period, the infant is expected to recover. Spitz also described this as an "emotional deficiency disease" (Spitz, 1965). The occurrence of an anaclitic depression was linked by Spitz to the "developmental milestone of the mother's becoming a consistent and recognized object for the infant" (Wagonfeld & Emde, 1982, p. 66). "Anaclitic" means "leaning upon", and in anaclitic depression the infant becomes depressed because the mother is not experienced as available to lean upon.

Anaclitic depression is related to the establishment of an object tie. Spitz emphasized that the children who develop anaclitic depressions are those who had once developed satisfactory object ties. A good object attachment must first be established in order for its loss to be mourned. Erikson (1950) spoke of the loss of maternal love as a cause of anaclitic depression, which he described as a "chronic state of mourning". He further speculated that infants and young children who suffer from the loss of the libidinal object during the second half of the first year might experience a depressive undercurrent for life.

Bowlby (1960) wrote of the effect of maternal loss on the developing infant and observed the sequence of protest, despair, and detachment behaviors from prolonged separation. Mahler (1968) understood anaclitic depression in terms of separation-individuation. She stated that after six months, once a symbiotic relationship with the mother has been established, she is no longer transposable, and her loss produces an anaclitic depression in the infant.

Many of the babies that Spitz observed died. I believe that those infants experienced "hopelessness". Without hope there is no will to live and we die. In the Greek myth of Pandora's box, Zeus put hope at the very bottom beneath all the evils in the world. Under greed, vanity, envy, and slander lay hope. "Sometimes, hope for the right thing can be reached only through an immersion in prolonged and harrowing dread" (Mitchell, 1993, p. 228). The babies that Spitz observed had become hopeless.

There is very little in the psychoanalytic literature about "hope" and "hopelessness", and almost nothing at all concerning children and hope and hopelessness. Boris (1976), one of the few who explored this topic, stated: "If one searches the literature hope itself is nowhere to be seen. This is no accident. Psychoanalysis is primarily a theory concerning desire and its vicissitudes." (Boris, 1976, p. 139) Boris conceived of hope as a psychological space where the self may find a new beginning. In Boris's theory, hope must first be given-up within the analytic experience, in order to experience despair. In Boris's mind, only then can one truly experience desire (Mitchell, 1993, p. 205).

Mitchell points out that psychoanalytic theory has approached hope from two opposing angels. The more traditional view is that hope is considered to be regressive and that it obstructs maturation and gets in the way of enjoying ones life experiences. The opposing viewpoint regards hope "as essentially progressive and facilitating of richer experiences" (Mitchell, 1993, p. 205).

Erikson (1950) and Winnicott (1989) wrote about hope in relation to children. Erikson connects the idea of hope and hopelessness to a *basic sense of trust* and a *basic sense of mistrust* that developmentally occurs in early infancy. If the infant's psychological and physical needs are met within reason, he learns to trust, and within this trust lies hope. Erikson views hope as progressive and growth enhancing, not regressive. Winnicott, in his work with acting-out adolescent boys, understood their difficult behaviors as an expression of hope. Winnicott, too, viewed hope as constructive and progressive. Winnicott, like Boris, saw regression as a vital characteristic of the therapeutic process but for Winnicott "regression has everything to do with hope" (Mitchell, 1993, p. 206).

Conclusion

Georgie shared his infantile hopes and feelings of hopelessness with me. In the analytic space old hopes were altered, and within the therapeutic relationship, new hopes took form. Before Georgie's analysis he was stuck. He could only express his intrapsychic pain through pathological symptoms. Georgie told me his story through inanimate objects that came apart easily and needed to be handled with care. As we played and pretended together new meanings developed and new possibilities opened up. Georgie experienced an infantile regression, which could be understood as defensive and pathological, but his painful regressive state could also be viewed as positive, hopeful communications. Mitchell reminds us that: "infantile hopes represent a self-healing return to the point at which psychological growth was suspended. Infantile hopes and longings do not need to be renounced but rather reanimated and brought to life, so they can grow and develop into more mature hopes through natural, organic maturational process." (Mitchell, 1993, p. 207)

For Georgie, life was fragile, his body was fragile, and his sense of self was almost non-existent as he did not feel human. He had to come to terms with the fragility of life. Growing up means acknowledging that the people you love the most, your parents, will eventually disappoint and let you down, and ultimately abandon you through death. "To love in a committed fashion, over time, is to hope; and to hope is to impart value in an inevitably uncertain future." (Mitchell, 1993, p. 212)

Georgie's analysis came to a premature and abrupt ending, thus we were never given the chance to accomplish all that needed to be done. Within our play space, Georgie remained a lifeless object; he was a car, or a marble, or a fragile transformer that fell apart easily. He was never a real boy. Georgie tried very hard to reach out to his father, who, although he attempted, never was able to understand or value Georgie's mind. Sometimes I wonder if Georgie will remember his promise in our last session, and I allow myself to imagine that one day, he will return to finish what we began.

PART II

MILDER PSYCHOPATHOLOGY

CHAPTER FIVE

The betrayed child

B ella, a leggy, seventeen-year-old beauty, slid gracefully into my office for her initial session. Her large luminous eyes hurriedly securitized her surroundings as she settled herself into the chair. Even though she was quite tall she gathered her legs under her and appeared as if a small child, bewildered to find herself in this place. Bella, an accomplished musician on full scholarship to a renowned music school, wanted to quit, giving up the dream of a promising professional career, a dream she had aspired to and wished for since she was a very young child when she first fell in love with her instrument.

At first Bella was wary of me and of therapy, especially psychoanalysis because a friend had told her that analysis was a terrible hoax, where the analyst "seduced" you into a "dependent" love, only to "abandon" you. "This," she emphatically exclaimed "is the ultimate betrayal!" This provocative statement enticed me, and I began to feel seduced by her as her story unfolded.

Seduction

In one of his etiological hypotheses, Freud (1895d, 1896c) proposed that all neuroses were caused by sexual seduction of children by adults.

This could vary from over-stimulation, visually and/or verbally, to physical sexual abuse. Freud's seduction hypothesis proposed that when a child was over-stimulated sexually (verbally, visually, or physically) by an adult, the result was anxiety and repression. Later, these repressed memories are triggered by an event, which leads to symptom formation (Akhtar, 2009). Freud believed, for example, that all of his hysterical female patients had experienced sexual trauma as children. As a result, their hysterical symptoms symbolized and communicated repressed traumatic sexual memories. Over time Freud came to doubt his seduction hypothesis and replaced it with a theory of intrapsychic causation. He purported that his hysterical female patients' "memories" of seduction were intrapsychic fantasies, which in turn were remnants of unconscious childhood wishes (Person & Klar, 1994).

This striking (although gradual) change from seduction in reality to intrapsychic childhood fantasies was pivotal in the evolution of psychoanalytic theory and technique. From then on, psychoanalytic ideas were grounded in the study of wishes and fantasies that derive from the unruly and anachronistic unconscious. In other words, exploring unconscious conflicts was the focus of psychoanalytic thinking and practice. Traumatic events in the lives of patients were no longer of consequence, which in turn diminished the significance of reconstructing childhood memories. Until recent years, most American analysts emphasized unconscious mental contents and their transformations as the chief interest of psychoanalysis. The focus has been on how these fantasies impact reality, but not the other way around. This is undoubtedly a one-person psychology (Person & Klar, 1994). However, Freud (1940a) continued to think of actual seduction as one possible cause of adult symptom formation and never gave up entirely on his seduction hypothesis (Blum, 2008).

As psychoanalytic theory evolved, some analysts gave up trying to reconstruct the past and accepted psychoanalysis as a hermeneutic science, while many others took the position that unconscious fantasies are impossible to differentiate from repressed memories. We know that memories are condensed and altered over time and are multiply determined as well as multi-layered with meanings. We also understand that prohibited fantasies and real experiences often merge, but nevertheless, actual trauma needs to be addressed. It is a painful reality that many children are seduced by their parents (Kramer & Akhtar, 1991; Gartner, 1997; Shengold, 1999; Colarusso, 2011). This is a sad and disturbing truth, which works to fortify the effects of the child's forbidden Oedipal fantasies (Greenacre, 1956). For this paper I will not address actual sexual abuse or incest, but instead will focus on the girl who has ostensibly won her Oedipal struggle. This is the girl who feels she is preferred over her mother by her father; the girl who feels she is given greater adoration than the mother: the girl who is *seduced* and *betrayed*.

Introducing Bella

Bella was the youngest of three girls. Her two sisters were ten and twelve years older than she. Both were married and highly successful in professional careers. Bella's father enjoyed acclaim and fame in his field, while her mother never worked outside of the home. Bella was clear that she was a "mistaken pregnancy" born to parents in their mid-forties. She described her mother as "exhausted", taking frequent naps throughout her childhood. She was a lonely little girl who retreated into elaborate make-believe play as her mother slept away the day. Bella longed for physical closeness with her mother, which she felt she had to "steal" from her while she slept. Bella told me in an early session: *I would tiptoe into her room because if I woke her she would chase me down the hall; so I was terrified of waking her. I would lie next to her and wrap my leg over her back while she slept. I loved that.* As Bella's story unfolded it became clear that she had been a creative, bright little girl who figured out that the only way to be close to her depressed, ineffectual mother was to join her in slumber. She turned to her father for emotional support, and he to her. In both of their eyes she was the most special daughter.

The role of the father

Freud did not deem the role of fatherhood particularly significant until the child reached the Oedipal phase of development. For Freud, it was the father's responsibility to establish the incest barrier (1909b, 1924d); almost a decade later he emphasized the father's role as that of protector (1930a). There was little interest in the role of fathers among psychoanalytic theorists until Loewald (1951) introduced the idea that the father must step in to prevent engulfment by the mother. Mahler and Gosliner (1955) "further elucidated the father's role in the development of the child's ego as well as his superego precursors" (Akhtar & Powell, 2004, p. 76). A decade later Mahler (1967) underscored the father as different from the mother in that he was more playful, while Benedek (1970) focused on the father's role and its effect on the child's personality development, and Abelin (1971) emphasized the important function the father has in helping the pre-Oedipal child separate from the mother (Akhtar & Powell, 2004). Following Abelin, Mahler et al. (1975) also declared that the father's job was to rescue the infant from her symbiotic bond to the mother. Mahler demonstrated, through child observational research, that as the child developed from infancy to toddlerhood, the father is differentiated from the mother and is seen as mystifying and stimulating. However, as much as the father is enjoyed, the "practicing" infant returns to the mother when in need of comfort or when upset, hungry, or tired. During the rapprochement sub-phase (sixteen months to thirty-six months), the father becomes more important to the toddler who begins to experience ambivalent feelings toward the mother. In this way, the father is essential in helping the toddler separate and individuate from the mother (Mahler et al., 1975). More recent theorists explain that during rapprochement, the little girl and her father share a mutual admiration. The child has a wish to identify with the father, which he supports and encourages (Benjamin, 1991).

Bella had no memories of playing with her mother or of being read to or held except when bathed. She came alive when she spoke of her father describing him as funny, loving, and extremely physical. In one particular session, eighteen months into her analysis, Bella was despondent over her career and her love life. She felt her musical career and her current boyfriend were lacking, frustrating, and unfulfilling. Bella had a series of men, whom she easily seduced, but just as quickly her feelings turned to abject distain and she rejected them. Her thoughts went to her father as she worried that he was disappointed in her. She longingly reminisced about her early childhood:

He was the best father. I know I was his favorite when I was little. When we went out to eat, he would tell the waitress that my mother was his mother and that I was his wife. It embarrassed me a little when I got older, but when I was really little I loved it. He said to me almost every day, let's kill your mother and run away and get married! It was a silly joke, but he said it all the time. I loved it. I would laugh. It was exciting. But now as I tell you about it, I'm embarrassed and I feel sad. I feel bad for my mother. It's sad.

As far back as Bella's memories go, she found herself in a predicament. She was an Oedipal victor.[1] Because of her mother's depression and emotional unavailability, she was unable to identify with or idealize her. She was forced to turn to her father. In response, her father encouraged this relationship as Bella provided the emotional closeness that he was not able to get from his wife. In such situations "fathers often turn to their daughters as surrogate spouses or mothers and then re-enact the separation-individuation conflicts of their own childhoods" (Kieffer, 2004, p. 76). For Bella, there seemed to be a pre-Oedipal narcissistic quality to her need to replace the mother.

Bella's Oedipal conflict

Let us imagine Bella from age three on. Her mother is asleep, passive and depressed, uninterested in, or unable to engage with her bright creative little girl. Her somewhat narcissistic father playfully seduces her into believing that she is favored over her sleeping mother. He jokes about killing off mother and marrying Bella often calling her his *wife* in public. In addition, Bella described her home environment as a *naked house* where bathroom and bedroom doors were left open, and baths and showers were shared. Bella often showered with her father until well into her latency years. Blum (1973) states: "parental seduction and exhibitionism undermine and corrupt superego development. There can be paradoxical permission and prohibition of sexual gratification by a superego modeled after contradictory parental behavior." (Blum, 1973, p. 67) Clearly Bella's overstimulating (father) yet depressed (mother) home environment affected many aspects of her development.

Back to theory

According to Freud (1908c), "penis envy" occurs when the pre-Oedipal girl discovers anatomical differences, feels inferior, and desires to have a penis. Because of her lack of a penis the little girl turns away from her mother and takes her father as a libidinal object. This gives way to the Oedipal complex, which is resolved when the little girl no longer wishes for a penis but instead wishes for a baby. Only then can she identify with her mother as a woman (Akhtar, 2009; Kieffer, 2004).

Not everyone agreed with Freud as to the little girls' entry into the Oedipal phase of development. Horney (1924, 1926) felt that penis envy was a "flight from womanhood" and was pathological, not a normal phase of development. In her view, penis envy develops when the Oedipal phase goes awry and the girl runs away from her libidinal connection to the father fearing competition with her mother. In Horney's view this is why the girl desires a penis as she identifies with the father (Horney, 1924, 1926).

Jones (1927, 1935) also disagreed with Freud, stating the "girl's attitude is already more feminine than masculine" (Jones, 1935, p. 265) as her "femininity develops progressively from the promptings of an instinctual constitution" (Jones, 1935, p. 273). Jones did not understand female sexual development to be based on a girl's disappointment in her genitals (Zetzel, 1960). Thompson (1954) spoke of a psychology of women that was not based on penis envy as the bedrock of female psychosexual development. Several other psychoanalysts understood the little girl's desire for the penis as a reaction against the fear of engulfment by the all-powerful, omnipotent pre-Oedipal mother (Chasseguet-Smirgel, 1970; Dinnerstein, 1976; Chodorow, 1978; McDougall, 1980). The term penis envy came to be associated with the idea that women are psychologically inferior to men which in turn altered psychoanalytic thinking, as many analysts no longer viewed conflicts of identity, narcissism, and aggression as "merely penis envy" (Barnett, 1966; Ewens, 1976; Grossman & Stewart, 1976). Lerner (1976), spoke of "parental mislabeling of female genitals" as a cause of grave psychological consequences resulting in the girl feeling like she has something less than the boy which contributes to the girl's penis envy. Lerner reasons, "penis envy is not really a wish for a penis … but rather may reflect the wish to validate and have 'permission' for female sexual organs" (Lerner, 1976, p. 269).

Parens et al. (1976) take a different theoretical pathway into the Oedipal complex for little girls. From their mother/infant research they observed that the girl's "wish to have a baby during the first genital phase does not necessarily follow upon or depend on the prior wish to have a penis" (Parens et al., 1976, p. 102). They further postulated that the little girl does not need to experience castration anxiety in order to enter into the Oedipal phase and that biological and maturational forces "thrust the girl into her Oedipal complex" (Parens et al., 1976, p. 103).

Freud described the Oedipus complex as occurring between three to five years of age, when the child copes with a multitude of confusing feelings in association with his parents. Most pronounced are erotic feelings for the opposite-sex parent, and rivalrous feelings with the same-sex parent. At the same time the child is fascinated with the mysteries of pregnancy and childbirth. "Successful negotiation of passage through the Oedipus complex results in the creation of the incest barrier, acceptance of generational boundaries, entry into the temporal dimension of life, respect for the value of waiting and effort, and formation of the superego." (Akhtar, 2009, p. 197) In addition, the child also needs to identify with the superego prohibitions of the "forbidding Oedipal parent" (Davies, 2003, p. 3). Loewald (1979) stated that the child needed to be able to mourn what he must relinquish and not repress these feelings. He stressed that when Oedipal guilt is repressed, a relentless pursuit of punishment results and enters into future relationships.

As stated above, with successful negotiation of the Oedipal phase, the incest barrier is established; however, this does not mean that "declarations of attractiveness" between parents and children are eliminated (Akhtar, 1994). Akhtar (1992) spoke of an "Oedipally-optimal distance that is neither incestuously intrusive nor oblivious of cross-generational eroticism" (Akhtar, 1994, p. 443). It seems clear that Oedipal development as well as its resolution is affected by both intrapsychic dynamics and the outside environment (Gill, 1987).

The child enters the Oedipal phase of development already influenced and shaped by her pre-Oedipal years (Abend, 1988). From memories as far back as age three we know that Bella's mother was depressed and for the most part, uninterested in her child. We can easily speculate that perhaps Bella's first three years were also with a very depressed mother. In Bella's early phase of her analysis she was constantly afraid that she was boring me stating that she worried I would fall asleep while she spoke. In her second year of her analysis, Bella became depressed and described her emotional needs as "disgusting". She worried I would be repelled by her needs and turn my back to her as her mother did when she was young. After many difficult months, she was able to call my message machine gaining comfort in hearing my voice and accepting a return call from me when needed. This transference of the depressed mother was excruciatingly painful as Bella often spent sessions silently weeping. It became clear that she needed me to speak to her at these moments to assure her that I had not fallen asleep. It was during this time that Bella lost the ability to maintain the "as-if" quality to our relationship. When the mother is emotionally unavailable or rejects and ignores her child's requirements, the child is unable to develop an efficient and adaptive method of communicating his or her needs. Very quickly a system of gross misattunement is set up which sets the stage for dysregulation and distress (Stern, 1985; Slade, 1998). As the mother recognizes and finds meaning in her child's affects, the child is then able to see herself as a thinking, feeling, separate self. When the mother is unable to contain and reflect her infant's affects the infant then becomes unable to self-regulate and normal development is at risk (Slade, 1998).

Stern defines attunement as the "intersubjective sharing of affect" (Stern, 1985, p. 141). Several developmental and attachment theorists (such as Bowlby, Ainesworth, Winnicott, Stern, & Karen) all consider attunement to be critical to the psychological and physical development of the infant. As the infant cries and demands to have his needs met, the mother responds and thus gives meaning to the infant's signals. Eventually the infant begins to know what he wants and how to signal with intent. This harmonized mother-infant *pas de deux* is a form of mutual regulation, and as a result the infant learns to regulate himself. First, the infant is able to self-regulate biological functions such as sleep patterns, elimination, and eating. Gradually, as the mother-infant dance continues to develop, the baby learns to self-regulate on a psychological level as well. Shared social experiences (such as playful interchange and mirroring) give the child a sense of being appreciated and cared for. His emotions and affects are accepted and validated. She feels approval. These early social experiences usher the child into the richness of object relations and what it means to relate to another person.

A depressed or otherwise compromised (e.g., battered, ill, drug-addicted) parent who does not have the capacity for self-reflection is unable to reflect on the inner states of her infant. This child will, in turn, be unable to relate to his own inner world. Attachment research has shown that insecurely attached adults tend to persist in strategies and schemas that they first learned from their own rejecting parent. In an effort to avoid an empty inner world devoid of objects, people incorporate malevolent inner objects. This loyalty to the early depriving caregiver causes a parent to continue rejecting patterns in her own interaction with her own children (Eagle, 1995; Karen, 1998). The infant who does not experience attunement and mirroring may experience her emerging preverbal self as defective. She is left to feel empty, helpless, and perhaps in severe cases, even without hope. Bella described herself as "defective", never feeling smart enough or talented enough. Perhaps this sense of a defective self is one reason why Bella believed her father's seduction and embellished it.

In order to navigate the Oedipal experience the child needs to have experienced good-enough pre-Oedipal years. This "requires a unified self with the capacity for intentionality, and objects which are experienced as distinct from oneself and towards whom ambivalence can be tolerated" (Akhtar, 1994, p. 443). Luckily Bella's father was able to step in for mother, but at a cost, for while he was attentive, and loving, he was also highly seductive and over-stimulating. Davies (2003) writes that the parent's love for the Oedipal child is steeped with healthy narcissistic adulation that she describes as "primitive" and "boundariless". She portrays the parent's love for the Oedipal child as "simply different; it is of a different order and type than love for the partner. It is more idealizing, more narcissistic, more visceral." (Davies, 2003, p. 9) Fenichel (1931) stated that the parent's unconscious sexual feelings and attachment for his child might become exceptionally strong when his sexual and emotional relationship with his partner is ungratifying (Fenichel, 1931). It seemed that Bella's father's own unsatisfied needs to be adored took over as he seduced Bella into thinking she was loved and desired more then her mother, which in turn had crucial consequences for her future development.

Unconscious Oedipal fantasies influence later life as they have an effect on symptom formation, character traits, and preferential means of gratification. "Love, jealousy, possession, envy, rivalry, rejection, ecstasy, disappointment, betrayal, power, helplessness, self-esteem, procreation, sexual roles, identity, triumph, defeat, guilt, revenge, restitution … preoccupy us for all the rest of our lives." (Abend, 1988, p. 502) Oedipal fantasies make the child vulnerable as her infantile narcissism is in full force. She wishes for the parent to pledge much more than he is realistically able to provide. "[T]he implicit parental promise is that sexually competitive wishes to win an exclusive, possessive relationship with the desired parent will be gratified if only the child wins the competition by playing by the imagined rules of the game." (Josephs, 2001, p. 705) Eventually the child realizes that at the end of the day, Daddy drives off into the sunset with Mommy, while she is left to go to bed alone in her own room. This is met with terrible disappointment but she comes to understand that no matter how flirtatious she is or how hard she tries to win the game, she will lose. From the child's perspective, the "Oedipal situation represents the tension between the child's first traumatic experiences of sexual/romantic exclusion from the parental relationship" (Davies, 2003, p. 9). The child must be able to cope with the realization that her fantasy of blissful romantic perfection with her parent of choice is a myth (Davies, 2003). It is at this time that the child begins to see and understand that her parents are loyal to one another and they share intimacy and sexual passion in which she is excluded. As this is realized, the child may have a "sense of being small, sexually and romantically impotent, even insignificant" (Davies, 2003, p. 10).

Talking of Bella again

From Bella's narrative, I surmise that she did not experience the necessary painful disappointments that accompany Oedipal resolution, but instead continued to believe that she had won Daddy while Mommy slept. Within the "father" transference, Bella demonstrated a feeling of entitlement, as it was not uncommon for her to demand to change her appointment time, expecting me to comply. At these times, she became enraged, insisting that her needs should come first, ahead of all my other patients. While Bella was not sexually abused, I would speculate that she experienced a type of sexualized seduction that left her feeling emotionally betrayed and affected her development.

Bella's post-Oedipal years—latency and adolescence—were also complicated. Now, we know that one of the main goals of post-Oedipal development is to be able to tolerate imperfections in oneself and in others. This requires a "mutual relinquishing of both the idealized other and the idealized self, in return for the experience of more deeply knowing and being known, being accepted for who one is, and discovering in oneself the capacity to love in spite of, and because of other's imperfections" (Davies, 2003, p. 12). Because of the trauma of having a depressed mother in her pre-Oedipal years creating narcissistic impairment and unresolved pre-Oedipal developmental conflict, Bella seemed to be stuck, never achieving the complex organization of tolerating ambivalence; simultaneously loving and hating the people she loved and depended on. In addition, post-Oedipally comes the ability to tolerate disappointment in ourselves and others and, most important, the capacity for intimacy through mutual vulnerability.

Bella's latency years were difficult as she struggled academically. She experienced difficulties with learning how to read, describing feelings of embarrassment and humiliation. Because of her high intelligence she compensated for what could have been an undiagnosed learning difficulty and figured out ways of "fooling" her teachers. It is also possible that Bella's overstimulating home environment prevented her from being able to sublimate as her latency stage of development seemed delayed. She was an outgoing little girl and made friends easily, although in late latency and pre-teen years she was bullied by a group of "mean" girls. These years were miserable, causing her to withdrawal from friendships. She found comfort in her music but at the cost of isolation. The loneliness she described as a five-year-old remained and was still present when she began her analysis. Bella would find her mother napping every afternoon when she returned home from school and she disappeared into her pretend world. In her sessions she often worried that others would discover that she was "stupid", especially me, and she had a recurring dream where her professors accused her of not belonging: *They were not fooled by my A grades.*

When she was seven years old, she was given a violin and it quickly became apparent that she was talented. By the time she was ten years old, she was practicing over three hours per day and began to dream of a performance career. The music woke her mother (both literally and metaphorically) as Bella realized that when she played her mother was animated and attentive. Her music brought her mother back to life and for the first time she felt special in her mother's eyes. From that moment on Bella knew that as long as she played the violin her mother would love her. It is interesting to note that while Bella struggled in school, playing a difficult instrument and learning the intricacies of music theory came easily to her. At age seventeen, when she first sought treatment, she struggled with not only giving up her own identity as a musician, but she also faced the threat of losing her mother's love once again. Bella was fearful that if she did not become an accomplished violinist her mother would once again turn away from her and fall asleep.

The loneliness that filled her earliest years was quasi-replaced with a passion and drive for her music and a quest for "perfection". Her pretend play of her childhood that had filled her afternoons developed into daydreams and fantasies of fame and success as a violinist but also of the "perfect" man who would adore her. Bella described herself as "boy crazy", always in love, always a flirt. She became sexually active at fifteen years old. Bella spoke lovingly of her first boyfriend. Their relationship seemed innocent and pure. She wanted to be with him constantly, missing music lessons, practicing with less interest. Bella longed to be a "normal" teenager. She wanted to "hang out", go to football games, and other perceived normal activities that were denied her. Both of Bella's parents were disturbed by this sudden change. Her mother made her feel guilty. Bella cried silently as she recalled this time. *She didn't really say anything. She just looked as if I had killed her. That if I didn't become this great violinist she would be mortally wounded.* Bella's father's reaction was strikingly different than her mother's. He withdrew all physical contact and became cold and distant. Many fathers experience discomfort when their daughters enter puberty. It is a known phenomenon that fathers may feel discomfort in managing their erotic feelings toward their adolescent daughter and may result in the father's withdrawal (Kieffer, 2004). At the time Bella thought his behavior was a reaction to her lack of interest in her musical career, however, in her analysis she came to understand his cold distancing as a reaction to her budding sexuality with her boyfriend.

As stated above, Bella fell in love at age fifteen. He was her first kiss as well as the boy she lost her virginity to. They were together for eight months when they first engaged in sexual intercourse. It was soon after that Bella lost interest in him and broke his heart. From then on she had a succession of boys and men much older than she. She spoke with contempt about the men she conquered. *It's so easy! It is just way too easy and they* all *say the exact same thing in bed* [she mimicked and imitated her numerous lovers]. *As soon as it is over I just want them gone forever. I no longer have any interest. They disgust me ... I think because of the mere fact that I can fool them. But the sad part is, I don't know any other way to feel close to them.* Bella exhibited a grandiose omnipotent self as she described her badly chosen sexual entanglements. Her grandiosity can be understood as a "defense against awareness that Oedipal victory is false" (Kohut, 1996, p. 318). I hypothesize that Bella's lack of an internalized good-enough, comforting mother resulted in her difficulties in tolerating frustration, poor impulse control in her interactions with men, fragile self-esteem, and unneutralized aggression (Blum, 1981). This left her inclined to develop sadomasochistic relationships as noted within the transference and in her relationships with men.

Why is the "seduced child" a "betrayed child"?

The act of seduction can have an overwhelming destructive effect on a child's intrapsychic stability and development. Greenacre (1956) warned that if the child's Oedipal fantasies are reinforced by a reality experience, the disorganizing effect is immense. The child may experience conscious and unconscious rage toward her seducer as well as feelings of guilt. The defense of repression is commonly induced which protects the individual from the incestuous meaning of the seductive behavior (Williams, 1987). When Bella began treatment she was unaware of her anger toward either of her parents, but instead was acting out in a sado-masochistic way with men and by threatening to destroy her musical career. Because betrayal at the hands of her father was experienced as a narcissistic injury; first his unfulfilled seduction of her as a little girl and then his withdrawal from her when she became sexually active, her turning her back on her musical talent may also be viewed as an act of revenge. Perhaps this was a way of finally winning although she would ultimately harm only herself. "To the extent parental betrayal remains a narcissistic injury, the child wishes to turn the tables on the parents by seducing and betraying them in revenge, thereby attaining a vindictive triumph." (Josephs, 2001, p. 706) I believe this behavior also served to help alleviate and cope with overwhelming depressive feelings.

When Bella became sexually active her aggression/anger was directed toward the men she seduced. This could be understood as identification with the aggressor but also an attempt to feel intimacy and to be loved. Bella's seductive fantasies, which she acted upon, seemed to be ego-syntonic as she rationalized and hoped that her sexual conquests would provide the ultimate bliss of winning the forbidden man for herself. One could imagine that this is a type of psychological agony, as this behavior seemed to be driven by shame, jealousy, and envy. We can further surmise that as Bella identified with the aggressor she developed a "seductive superego", which "unconsciously arranges a tragic downfall for those who posses the hubris to believe that they can triumph in transgression" (Josephs, 2001, p. 702). Bella's defensive structure was to seduce and betray over and over before these men could seduce and betray her.

Bella began her analysis with the strong conviction that I would grossly disappoint her. She claimed I would seduce her into dependency and then abandon her leaving her feeling only disappointment and betrayal. Her presenting problem when she sought treatment was an overarching disappointment in everything in her life, specifically her romantic relationships and her music. In other words, there was an air of non-fulfillment about Bella that seemed to be both defensive and aggressive. Many people feel a sense of disappointment when life experiences do not meet wishes and expectations.

Bella often spoke of her experiences as not living up to her expectations. Her performances were never good enough; she never played well enough in rehearsal or in her private sessions with teachers. Most striking, her relationships with men were never what she had imagined or hoped for. She entered her analysis profoundly steadfast to the idea of being disappointed in her analyst and her analysis as a whole. Throughout the early years of treatment she tried over and over to seduce me into loving her, whereby she would quickly turn me into a disappointment who could never meet her expectations. She either saw me as her father who promised her everything and delivered nothing, or her mother who turned her back and fell asleep. In both of these scenarios, she worked hard to bring out the worst in me, as I became the bad object who always let her down. Bella's dilemma was that if she became vulnerable and allowed herself to experience intimacy with her analyst she ran the risk of engulfment, yet to reject me left her alone.

I understood Bella's use of disappointment as a defense against very early memories of recurrent disappointments and loss. After all, her father promised her daily to *kill her mother and run away together*. When she became interested in boys and entered into an age-appropriate relationship, her father rejected her by demonstrating displeasure and withdrawal of physical contact. The emotional abandonment by her depressed mother was extremely damaging as she was insecurely attached, had difficulty developing object constancy, and suffered from separation anxiety. In addition Bella carried the guilt of winning her father's admiration away from a depressed sleeping woman. Schafer (1999) notes: "Many patients who develop fixed, hardened attitudes of disappointment have suffered prolonged, severe deprivation and pain in their early object relations." (Schafer, 1999, p. 1,095)

Psychoanalysis thinks of the superego as the compass of an individual's moral development and manager of affects and behavior. The development of the superego has long been understood as a byproduct of progressing through the Oedipal phase of development. It is also thought that the superego is shaped by the attachment dynamic: "What is 'permissible' and 'good' is determined as much by the vicissitudes of the need for security as by rivalries and regulations of the oedipal triangle." (Holmes, 2011, p. 1,228) Certainly, a major job of the superego is to oversee limits and boundaries. Early on in development the superego is harsh and is limited to *good* and *bad*. However, as the individual matures and moves through developmental phases, the mature superego is more subtle and forgiving. Holmes adds that the development of a healthy, mature superego is dependent on an "internalized parent-child relationship that maintains safety" (Holmes, 2011, p. 1,238). As noted earlier, Bella was insecurely attached to her mother, which set up "narcissistically derived ego ideals-doomed to disappointment when confronted with reality" (Holmes, 2011, p. 1,229).

A seductive superego is defined as a "superego that rationalizes the gratification of prohibited impulses and renders them ego syntonic. This is, however, followed by humiliating punishment." (Akhtar, 2009, p. 257) It seemed that Bella had developed a seductive superego, which served to re-traumatize her as she set up seductions and betrayals in almost all of her relationships. Akhtar calls this phenomenon a "betrayal trauma upon the self and repeats similar betrayals by parents during childhood" (Akhtar, 2009, p. 257).

Some final remarks

For Bella, winning an "Oedipal victory" was a great disadvantage as her father's special treatment of her was both misunderstood by her and not genuine, given its base in his narcissism, leaving her with a sense of betrayal. She received a great deal of admiration from her father, but at an enormous cost to her development. When she entered her analysis at age seventeen, she was able neither to enjoy a mature sexually gratifying relationship nor to pursue her career. She expected to be disappointed in everything she did: her relationships, her career, and especially her analyst and analysis. I believe this was directly related to the loss of her seductive relationship with her father whom she idealized. Kieffer (2004) suggests, "that the favored daughter's position is maintained only by a continued dependence on father as a source of self-esteem" (Kieffer, 2004, p. 73). Bella identified with her father as she re-enacted seduction and betrayal in every romantic relationship. I speculate, supported by her analytic material, that Bella felt such overwhelming guilt by winning her father's love at the expense of her depressed mother that she brought about her own punishment in her love life and also by attempting to destroy her musical career.

Bella longed for a mother who would love and nurture her, while she was simultaneously riddled with guilt, blaming herself for her mother's lack of engagement. Only when she played music did her mother seem to see her. Bella came to realize that she worried that she was somehow hurting her mother by playing so beautifully, for being successful. She came to understand that by becoming a successful musician she was competing with her mother once again. Earlier in this paper I commented that Bella identified with her father. It became clear in our work together that she was also very much identified with her mother. Within this identification with mother, Bella often devalued herself as seen in her music and in her relationships. This was played out within the transference as she denigrated and demeaned herself in an effort to punish herself, while keeping me interested.

Bella's analysis was terminated prematurely when she accepted an offer to join an orchestra in Europe. While it was clear to both Bella and myself that we had further work to accomplish, we were both satisfied that she was in a much better position to move forward with her life. Just as normal development is never linear, neither was Bella's development into mature love. Just as it felt we might be entering into a post-Oedipal transference, she would once again idealize me and demand undying attention and love. I became the idealized love object only to disappoint her with my shortcomings. Slowly, Bella was beginning to cope with and accept the unattainability of her wishes, and she no longer had to seduce and betray others.

CHAPTER SIX

The greedy child

Violet Beauregarde, the overindulged young girl in the popular children's book *Charlie and the Chocolate Factor* (Dahl, 1964), insists upon "acquiring" an elf (an "Oompa-Loompa") for herself. She refuses to take no for an answer. Her fate is an unhappy one when she defies warnings and demonstrates oral greed as she shoves a gobstopper into her already overfilled mouth. Violet turns purple, and blows up into a giant grape. Her ending is not pretty, as she is rolled away to the juicing room protesting loudly, where she is to be "juiced" by the very Oompa-Loompa she demanded to posses. Veruca Salt, the other greedy girl character in the story, is a spoiled entitled child who demands everything, as she whines, "I want! I want! I want!" Veruca is given everything she wants, and takes what is not given, and what is not hers for the taking. When she insists that she be given a golden egg, the Oompa-Loompas determine that she is a "rotten egg" and Veruca is propelled down the garbage shoot where all the "bad" eggs must go. Augustus Gloop, one of two greedy male characters, is described as "enormously fat" as he refuses to listen and must binge on sweets. He, too, meets a grim end when he dives head first into a chocolate river and is sucked down the drain. Mike Teavee, the second greedy male character, is only content when he is watching television. He is thrilled to be dissolved into tiny particles and transported into the TV where he can have everything he ever wanted. Only Charlie, the hero of the story, is portrayed as a child, who has his greed in check. Charlie is not perfect; he, too, cannot deny temptation and takes something he is not allowed to have, but he can control his greediness, is apologetic for stealing, and is grateful for the few material things he has. The author, Roald Dahl, makes it clear that the parents of the overly greedy children are not able to help their children or love them in the way they need to be loved, while Charlie is born into a family where there is barely food on the table, but an abundance of love. In the end, Charlie wins the prize; he gets the whole chocolate factory. The moral of the story: nothing good will come of overly greedy children.

Melanie Klein (1952) locates greed in the oral stage of development, highlighting that greed is intensified by depravation, but stresses that there is a dynamic interplay between the innate aggressive drive and actual depravation. Klein states: "children in whom the innate aggressive drive is strong, persecutory anxiety, frustration, and greed are easily aroused" (p. 62). When loving feelings prevail between the mother and her infant, then the child is able to feel gratitude toward the loving object. However, when there is gross misattunement and when the libido-aggression balance within the dyad (and in the infant's intrapsychic world) is tilted towards aggression, then receiving supplies stirs up more hunger and more anger; this angry hunger constitutes greed.

Anna Freud (1965) describes how the young infant appears to possess an insatiable "oral greed" as she takes everything she desires. Greed by definition is inherently insatiable and will not be satisfied. When we call someone "greedy", we are disapproving and scornful. It is often said in annoyance and accompanied by an irritated tone (Boris, 1986). Harold Boris and Anna Freud do not view "greed" as pejorative, but rather as "an unresolved state of mind in which one wishes and hopes to have everything all of the time" (ibid., p. 45). By the beginning of the second year when the toddler acquires the use of the word "mine", "he begins to guard his possessions fiercely and jealously against any interference" (Freud, 1965, p. 117). Anna Freud points out that the concept of being stolen from comes into play much earlier than the understanding that the other's belongings are not for the taking, and in fact, "oral greed, anal possessiveness, urges to collect and horde, overwhelming need for phallic symbols, all turn young children into potential thieves unless educational coercion, superego demands, and with these, gradual shifts in id-ego balance work in the opposite direction, namely, toward the development of honesty" (pp. 117–118).

Winnicott (1986) also does not view greed as bad, but instead describes greed as a primitive love "that we are all frightened to own up to, but which is basic in our natures, and which we cannot do without" (p. 170). I imagine that the fantasy and wish to have every need met instantly and have everything all of the time is also a primitive wish to merge with the mother which produces a state of feeling high excitement and pure bliss.

The analysis of a greed-filled seven-year-old girl

Seven-year old Kay was brought for treatment because of night terrors, bed-wetting, and impulsive aggressive behaviors towards adults, other children, and small animals. Kay witnessed domestic violence, and on multiple occasions, her father threatened to kill his wife and abduct his children. When Kay was an infant, her mother burned Kay's esophagus by heating her bottle in a microwave oven. Kay's mother was obsessed with cleanliness and would wash the inside of Kay's vagina with a washcloth. When Kay was four years old through age seven, she suffered a chronic yeast infection where her perineum would sometimes become so raw it would bleed. Kay had also been told by both of her parents that she was stupid, worthless, and fat. Kay's parents lost custody of their child and the paternal grandparents took over her care and quickly sought psychoanalytic treatment.

The beginning

In her first session, this pretty, slightly overweight little girl, with enormous sad green eyes, stood in the center of my playroom, unable to move, seemingly paralyzed with fear. I stood near her and explained that in this room she could do whatever she wished. Within minutes after my encouragement, Kay became bossy and demanding, insisting, in an abrasive and somewhat cruel tenor, that I sit next to her at the dollhouse and make up a story. She was unable to take part in the play, but instead became the audience to my production of her commands. In subsequent sessions she continued her imperious and taxing demeanor. The play quickly turned to abusive mother/baby pretend. Session after session I was told that my child got lost and I could not find her; my baby was screaming in hunger and I was unable to obtain food; my baby was sick and I was inept at getting help. As the months went on this theme remained but became more elaborate. Through this painful "play" she showed me the abuse she had experienced since infancy. She quickly went to her hurt and her pain. Kay gave herself a character and demonstrated how she used splitting as a defense against her pathological greed by sometimes being the "good" Helen and sometimes the "mean" Helen. However, she continued to participate from outside of the play. By this I mean that she narrated the story and I had to speak the lines of my character, but her character never speaks. For example she would say: "Pretend that mean Helen hates you and gets all the townspeople to hate you, and your husband likes me better than you." I act out my despair and sadness and hurt over such treatment. Her response is: "Pretend Helen doesn't care."

The early phase of treatment

As the months wore on, Kay continued to have trouble connecting with other children her age or maintaining any type of meaningful relationships. She acted out aggressively and was bossy, manipulative, nasty, and extremely greedy both outside and in her analytic hour.

In her play she showed me over and over how devastated she felt under her grandiose disguise. She always put me in her place, as she frustrated, tricked, manipulated, controlled, and humiliated me. She slowly began to tolerate the profoundly sad feelings that I expressed (in the play), but would quickly change the theme of the play when she was no longer able to tolerate my affect. For example:

K: *Pretend that nobody likes you and you have no friends and you try to be my friend.* [I act this out and she rejects and ignores me and will not allow me to be her friend.]

A: *I feel so bad. I am so sad. I feel so alone. It is terrible that no one loves me. All I want is for somebody to love me.*

She watched me, but in a sideways fashion, out of the corner of her eye, while demanding that I repeat the whole scene several times. Eventually these themes overwhelmed her and she would attempt to change the play to an unrelated theme, but this always failed as she ended up rejecting and hurting me in every game. I would be exiled to a corner of the playroom as she screamed at me chanting hurtful slurs and stating clearly that I was completely unlovable. These games were repetitive and tedious and I was left to feel devalued and helpless. At the end of our first six months of her analysis, she began to act kindly toward me at the very end of the session. We had begun a ritual where, when I told her it was almost time to end, she would help herself to mints that I kept in my desk drawer. Perhaps she worried that I would not give her a mint if she were not nice. One mint was never enough. Kay would graciously accept the one mint I offered and then quickly grab as many as she could and run for the door. She had to take everything I had and what I gave her was never enough.

Kay elicited strong countertransference as her demeanor was extremely obnoxious, manipulative, and unpleasant. Understanding my countertransference was very important in working with her. I often felt bored, sleepy, humiliated, frustrated, irritated, and worthless. I felt that I was reacting to the emptiness in this little girl. It was as if she were dead, as if her soul had been murdered. However, for the most part, I was able to feel empathy for the pathetic, devastated little girl that she had buried underneath her nasty, greedy exterior.

After one year

Even though all of her presenting problems persisted in her outside world, I had a sense we were making progress. She had become more fluid in her play, would speak more readily about an event in her life such as a visit to her parents, and was able to tell me, *You feel really sad* instead of making me insert the affect into the play. For example, in our "mean Helen" game, she would take everything from me, my husband, my children, and all of my worldly goods, and instead of waiting silently for me to react, she would tell me what to feel: *I have everything you have nothing! I get it all you get nothing! You feel really really bad!*

Kay's play continued to be monotonous and repetitious. The point of the play seemed to be to take everything from me, to keep everything for herself, and to frustrate me. For example, she set up a parking game using matchbox cars. The whole play consisted of making sure I never got a parking spot. She did this through trickery. Her demeanor remained bossy, demanding, and controlling. She often screamed at me in a high-pitched voice to do her bidding. I interpreted how important it was to her to treat me this way and I wondered out loud if she is

treated this way in the real world. As she listened to my words, her features softened and she got a far away look in her eyes, perhaps sadness.
These interpretations were not responded to verbally but I felt that she
was taking in my words.

Kay continued to act out her real-life dramas as she insisted that I act
as an abusive mother who does not care for the welfare of her child.
I am told to hit and demean my child, leave my child home alone sitting in her excrement and at one point she wanted me to kill my child
by drowning her in the ocean. At times she would join me and we were
two terrible mothers who would go off shopping with our boyfriends.
Her identification with her mother's lying and deceit was evident in her
saying: *Pretend that we smile and seem happy in the stores. People can't tell
how mean we really are. Let's pretend that we can take anything in the store we
want, and nobody can stop us.*

In another continuing drama, I am the little sister who lives with
mean terrible parents. She is the big sister who has escaped. She has a
loving husband and two beautiful babies with whom she is very nurturing. She sends me a letter telling me I must sneak out in the middle
of the night and fly on an airplane to her home. She sends me the plane
tickets and $50,000. The game ends when I escape; she was unable to
continue the game where there would be a loving relationship between
the two of us. In this drama she was telling me her story, one of escape
to a safer home, but one where she still feels alone and isolated. Through
the transference her greed, hate, and envy were worked through as this
drama was replayed for many sessions.

Over time, Kay began to play a lot of school and teacher games. This
play demonstrated the many levels of our relationship and her improved
ego functioning. This play was used as another avenue, which she used
to feel superior to me, as she was the better teacher, the most loved
teacher, the smarter teacher, while I was left demeaned and alone with
nothing. At times she used this play as a way to distance herself from me,
perhaps as a defense against her fear of intimacy. At other times this play
demonstrated her move into latency as she acted out age-appropriate
scenarios where she followed rules and began to tolerate losing or not
having everything all of the time. As Kay's development improved
she became much more open verbally. She told me of her accomplishments in swimming and basketball. She spoke about situations while
visiting her parents in which she was upset and unhappy. She told me
when her grandparents punished her and how she outsmarted them.

She seemed to become a bit less greedy. In the past she had to use all the clay or all the paint or take all my mints from my desk. She began to show less compulsion to have it all and many times left sessions without depleting me of all I had. The fact that she no longer needed to rob me of my possessions in order to feel close to me indicated the growth of trust in our relationship. I began to think that perhaps I was beginning to become internalized as a new developmental object and that she had begun to have some "object constancy" (Mahler, Pine, & Bergman, 1975), and thus no longer felt compelled to take a part of me home with her. This improvement also demonstrated new ego-strength where she was better able to control her impulses. In addition, her hate, rage, greed, and envy were becoming modulated through our experiences together as she saw that these overpowering affects would not destroy our relationship, as she no longer needed to completely deplete me in order to feel okay.

The treatment deepens

Sexual themes entered our sessions as she began to bring questions about her feminine identity into her treatment. For example, she began a session by opening up a toy cell phone, removing the batteries, which had leaked, and washing out the interior of the phone. She used the phone to call a boyfriend who told her that he loved her. Next she made a tunnel out of a toilet paper roll to drive little cars through. Later in the session as we were constructing Valentines she told me: *Once I stuck a scissor in myself on purpose.*

She is unable to elaborate and changes the subject. She ended that session making necklaces for her siblings out of beads and she said: *I have a secret drawer where I keep all the things you have made me. If you come to my house I will let only you see inside my drawer.* In later sessions she spoke about a boy who dressed as a girl and how she is excited by a particular boy who kisses girls on the playground. In all of these interactions I listened. If I had interpreted her erotic feelings in a more adult manner she would have shut down limiting the possibility for further exploration.

All of Kay's play themes demonstrated her intense grandiose fantasies that covered up terrible insecurities. Her need to be admired and lauded was a thin camouflage for her inner feelings of chronic emptiness and boredom. She was in constant search for beauty, wealth, brilliance, and power. She was in search of the perfect "all-good" object. Her play and behavior was exceptionally controlling, which I understood as Kay's way of showing me that she felt helpless, controlled, and power-less. This left little room for capacity to love and to experience empathy for others. She often behaved in exploitive and ruthless ways toward her grandparents, siblings and her analyst. She successfully inflicted narcissistic injuries on others that she was terrified of suffering herself. Kay's play themes displayed her possessiveness, envy, jalousies, greed, and her impulses to kill rivals and frustrating figures had the potential of becoming nuclei for later dissociality. However, on Valentine's Day, I found a tiny Valentine that she left on the floor in my waiting room for me to find at the end of my day. This tiny glimmer of light gave me hope for further progress.

Kay's play gradually began to change. The monotonous, frustrating games of the previous year disappeared. She became more organized and contained. Her play became more creative as we built roads that had tollbooths that sent us off to magical destinations. However, even in this more advanced, creative play she made sure that I did not have enough money to get to the best most magical places. It seemed that her anxiety had diminished as she worked through her traumatic history, which allowed her creativity to come to the forefront. However, her envy and greed were still evident. A turning point in our work occurred when she began a game in which I was a queen and she my daughter/princess. In this role-play she sat close to me and called me "Queen Mommy" as we made invitations to her royal birthday party. This play, which continued in different forms, represented an important change in the transference from the "bad" mother transference to the "good" mother transference. My countertransference also began to change as I felt caring, warm feelings for her. This shift occurred because of her increased capacity for greater intimacy. She could now reverse the roles and accept a "loving mother". For the next several months, school games dominated, but an important change took place. I was given the role of head teacher and she is now my daughter and my assistant. For months we work together in a warm cooperative manner playing this game where we teach our children. Kay directs this play and we have music where we sing, art where we make creative projects, and academ-ics where our children may make a mistake, but we never ridicule or hurt their feelings. In our pretend recess time in our school game she makes up a game called "silent ball" with many rules, which she writes out on paper and hangs on the wall. Some of our children are unable to follow the rules and they are given consequences with warmth and understanding. These games indicated that Kay was moving forward developmentally and had entered her latency phase.

Kay began to bring me objects from home to share with me. When Kay began treatment she presented with a lack of gratitude and defects in the ability to express and feel empathy for others. At this point there was a shift as she began to acknowledge that she had received something good from me. At Easter, she gave me a basket of tulips and suggested that they could also be Passover flowers, adding that her grandfather thought that maybe I was Jewish. Around this time, she became interested in me and wondered how old I was, filling the white board with numbers and playing a guessing game to figure out my age. In subsequent sessions she probed, asking me other personal details about my life. She wondered if I am married, if I have children, and what kind of house I lived in. As I helped her explore her feelings toward me, she began to speak about herself and her family, but her inquisitive stance was an indication that she has begun to not only use me as a new developmental object and a transferential object, but was also viewing me as a real person with a mind of my own. She was no longer consumed by greed and envy, as she seemed to now be able to experience loving feelings.

Working through

As her analysis proceeded, the school game gained a variation on a theme. Sometimes we owned a pet store; sometimes a daycare, sometimes a restaurant or bakeshop. In all of these games, which became elaborate and filled the whole session, there were exact rules, regulations, and proper ways of behaving. Most importantly she fully included me (I no longer felt bored or sleepy), and she was no longer bossy, demeaning or humiliating toward me. The following segment of a session illustrates her latency-appropriate behavior and how Kay's ego functions had improved. She began her session by showing me her new outfit and new shoes and suggested I too, should go to this store and get new shoes for only $6.99. She set up school and stated that today will be Fun Day as she listed games we could play on the board. She settled on Dodge Ball and for the next thirty minutes we play this very physical game. She is very good at it, much better than I, and she played by the rules and was fair. She clearly enjoyed hitting me with the ball and became excited and over-heated.

A: *I think you are enjoying this game very much. It seems that you like hitting me with the ball.*
K: *I do! I do!*
A: *It also seems to be very important to you that you are better at this than I am.*
K: *Yes, yes. I like being better at this game!*
A: *This is a very exciting game and you are getting very excited.*

After I said this she told me it was nighttime and we needed to sleep. She made a bed on the floor and we lay down together. She said she was going to have a dream.

K: *I'm going to dream that I go to an island that is made out of ice cream and I can eat all the ice cream I want.*
A: *What a wonderful place. Who else is there?*
K: *You and me and my baby and you can eat all the ice cream you want and so can my baby.*
A: *The baby too?*
K: *It's a dream silly. Anything can happen in a dream! Now go to sleep!*

In our game we sleep past the alarm and have to hurry to school where we teach the children about fire drills. She is kind and nurturing as she helps the children to not be afraid of the shrill alarm that she confided in me scared her. At the end of the session she tells me she was exhausted from our play and crawled under the easel where she discovered there was a small blackboard and wrote "No Boys Allowed" and instructed me not to read it until after she has left. The above vignette demonstrates Kay's newfound capacity to feel empathy for others and her ability to be giving to others and not feel totally depleted in the giving. Also, as stated above, this session shows her entrance into age appropriate play and latency-feelings about boys.

After months of sessions like the above vignette, her bossy, greedy meanness came back. This regression was not unexpected as there are always ups and downs and reworking of the traumas, conflicts, and the transference. Once again, I was left helpless, rejected and abandoned in the play. This game was short-lived and after ten minutes of this regressed play she announced:

K: *Enough of this. Let's play school.*

However, in her school game I was left out again as we pretended that my children do not like me and leave me for her. She sent me from the school, never to come back. I was banished to a corner of the playroom.

A: *This feels sad. I'm all alone. Nobody seems to love me.*

She needs me to repeat this over and over and this scenario continued until the end of the session. She refused to help clean up and in a two-year old whiney voice announced that she refused to leave and could not understand why she just could not stay all day! I addressed her difficult feelings, verbalizing how one day she can feel very grown-up, competent, and loving and the next all of the difficult mean feelings come flooding back. These play scenarios demonstrated what Akhtar (2014) has underscored about greed: "The individual afflicted with it is momentarily pleased with the attainment of supplies and then becomes unsatisfied, empty, and inconsolable" (p. 37). In Kay's regressed state, it was helpful to remember Winnicott's (1986) wisdom: "If we acknowledge the importance of greed in human affairs, we shall find more than greed, or we shall find that greed is love in a primitive form. We shall also find that the compulsion to attain power can spring from fear of chaos and uncontrol." (p. 213) In her next session she went back to her newer behaviors as our games proceeded. Her grandiosity and sense of entitlement did not reappear until termination when it got replayed but with an important difference.

Termination

We decided to terminate for two reasons: the first was (as with many child cases) a necessity due to schedule and geographical distance. Kay needed to attend full day school. She was entering the fourth grade and it would be detrimental to her further development both academically and socially if she was not allowed to attend school like the other children. Because her grandparents traveled an hour and a half to bring her to me it became evident that my schedule (and hers) would not permit this arrangement to continue. I had maintained an intensive relationship with the grandparents since the beginning of treatment, meeting with them twice monthly. These meetings, while difficult at times, had proved extremely beneficial as the grandparents valued my advice and worked very hard to help their granddaughter. I was confident that Kay had grown very close with her grandmother in particular and this woman was providing a secure, loving holding environment for Kay to continue healing.

I had begun an analysis with Kay because her normal progressive development had been arrested. Kay's clinical material suggested very clearly that she was back on track developmentally. This was supported by reports from the grandparents that her acting out behaviors had stopped at home and at school, the night terrors were gone and she no longer wet the bed. She was better able to understand her living situation and was coping better with her visits to her parents. She could now verbalize her fears, sadness, and tremendous anger, and she could speak about her disappointments in the parents she loved so much. At first Kay was displeased with the decision to end, but comforted with the choice to maintain one session per week. In almost every session during this ending period she went back to a play/drama from early in our work but with a significant difference, the endings were altered. She replayed the scenario of the poor abused little sister who needed to escape from her parents. The game was exactly as we played it over a year ago except when we got to the end. Now, she accepted me into her home and off we went shopping together. In this play Kay retold her story, but now she felt intimate with me. She no longer felt abandoned, alone, and isolated. In another session she replayed some of her earliest games wherein she built a car lot in the sand. The game retained some of its original monotony where I began to feel left out, bored and sleepy, when she suddenly included me. In yet another session, she replayed a game where we were college students and I saw her from afar and I was bedazzled by her beauty. I am so taken with her that I followed her home and asked to be her friend because she was so beautiful, owns a magnificent home, and has the most expensive car. When we played this game a year ago, she would end up rejecting and ignoring my desire to befriend her and the game would end with her being very nasty to me. This time she accepted my friendship; we became best friends who had wonderful husbands and beautiful babies. In all of these dramas, Kay was retelling her story, but with new endings. She no longer felt as worthless and unlovable as she did when we began. Her grandiosity and greed remained to a degree and she continued to be easily narcissistically wounded, but her coping capacity had been greatly fortified.

In one of our final sessions we played school once again. I was the teacher and she my student. She insisted that I give her difficult math problems, reading comprehension, and spelling tests. In the past she would refuse to take any risk where she might fail. She could not tolerate the humiliation of being wrong. I was amazed as she attempted difficult problem solving and was able to ask for help and was not mortified when she made a mistake. At the end of the session she spoke of her excitement about going away with her parents on a vacation to another state to visit relatives, and her worries that school may be difficult this year.

Discussion

Kay had experienced abuse and neglect by her primary attachment figures. I speculate that Kay's mother, who was not at all attuned to her infant daughter's physical discomforts, could not provide emotional attunement. Kay's mother was unable to act as an auxiliary ego in order to support her infant's immature and unstable ego functions. Kay began life at risk, and learned early on that her world was an uncomfortable and hostile place.

There was some salvation for Kay, in that she had grandparents to stand-in and provide for her emotional and physical needs during infancy and her pre-Oedipal years. I conjecture that she got enough nurturance to enable her to continue to develop in certain areas, as evidenced by her advanced academic skills. Between the ages of five years through seven years, during her Oedipal years, she lived with her parents. During these years she experienced confusing physical and emotional abuse. These early impingements had the effect of disrupting Kay's ego integration, her sense of self, and her object relations. These early traumas led to a premature and pathological (although adaptive) narcissistic defensive organization. As an abused child she felt unlovable and worthless. She had internalized self-with-other as "bad" and "dangerous". She demonstrated what her experiences had been with adults in her life by splitting and being either all good or all bad. Kay's defense of splitting was maintained because of her rage toward her mother and father. She was unable to integrate and resolve both hating and loving her parents. Kay developed pathological narcissistic defenses to avoid feeling intense and unbearable pain and sadness. It is also my belief that her narcissistic self-formation, plus her free-floating sadism may have protected her from developing a major depression. As stated above, Kay's early traumas and maltreatment have interfered with the development of her ego and it's functions. This, in turn, influenced her adaptation to her environment. Her coping mechanisms suggested severe pathology as she had retreated into grandiosity and omnipotence as a defense against her poor self-esteem and her lack of trust in others. Kay demonstrated her understandably skewed sense of self, and her understandably intense need for my admiration, over and over in her games that demanded that I find her beautiful, smart, and powerful.

Kay suffered emotional and physical deprivation leaving her virtually starving, which in turn caused her to continuously search for anything and everything to fill her emptiness. Akhtar (2014) states: "The child then pushes the envelope of supplies, takes a lot, steals from his caregivers, and behaves in outrageous ways." (p. 45) In addition her infantile omnipotence appeared untamed (Blum, 1991). When Kay stole from me, I understood this behavior as her need to "compensate [herself] for the earlier deprivation but also to hurt the benefactor who has come to stand for the depriving primary objects" (Winnicott, 1986, p. 45).

Considering the severe trauma that Kay experienced, why did she improve so dramatically in a relatively short period of time? The answer is multiply determined. As soon as Kay's grandparents obtained legal custody they actively sought psychoanalytic treatment. They had deep concerns for their granddaughter and made a great effort to obtain the best treatment they were able to afford. They were supportive of the treatment and developed a positive working alliance with me. They were able to tolerate the intense relationship that develops between the patient and the analyst. It should also be noted that they made Kay's analysis a top priority, driving a great distance and altering school schedules. The grandparents attended parent sessions with me twice monthly and highly valued my advice and guidance. Slowly over time they altered their behavior and Kay's home environment significantly improved. Kay was court-ordered to have scheduled visitations with her parents. What became immediately imperative was that the grandparents needed guidance in how to handle these visits and how to get along with their estranged son and his wife. Improvement was notable when the grandparents began to accept and understand Kay's ambivalent feelings for her parents. It was difficult for them to comprehend that Kay had loving feelings for parents who had been so abusive to her. I was surprised and impressed when the grandmother began to relate positive loving stories to Kay about her father when he was a little boy. Most important and helpful was the fact that the grandparents no longer "trashed" Kay's parents when they began to understand that this was extremely damaging to Kay's self-esteem and reinforced the splitting that Kay was already expressing. It was also difficult for the grandparents to understand the necessity of appropriate limit setting for Kay. Part of this trouble was because they were her grandparents and very much enjoyed the grandparent role; however over time, they came to understand that it was detrimental to Kay's development when there were loosely defined boundaries. Kay's grandparents understood that setting rules and limits and providing appropriate boundaries helped Kay begin to self-regulate. They heeded my concern, that left unchecked, Kay had the very real potential to develop an "addictive disorder-such as abuse of alcohol or drugs, or promiscuous, hyperactive sexuality-or tendencies toward exploitative manipulations of others, theft, and other delinquencies" (Blum, 1991, p. 296).

Kay, herself, demonstrated superior intelligence, creativity, and the ability to make use of symbolism and metaphor. I feel that Kay's innate intelligence and other strengths drove the therapy, particularly in our enactments, but given such a dramatic improvement over a two-year period, what led to progress was the working through of her trauma through reconnecting to the object. Through the use of the mirroring transference Kay could really see herself in our work. Mirroring of the child-as-victim but also victim-as-child was valuable. This was done by submitting myself to the process of working through over and over and over again. Intensive work with the grandparents combined with Kay's innate superior intelligence and other character strengths made Kay analyzable so the work could proceed.

However, the treatment as a whole was most responsible for her improvement. I became a new empathic developmental object and provided a safe play space where Kay was able to work through her traumatic experiences. She was able to make use of me as a new developmental object as well as a real object. She was able to tolerate my interpretations that linked her traumatic experiences to her reactions within the play and integrate them into her new developing sense of self. Trust in our relationship grew and she became confident that I would accept her no matter how terrible she treated me within the metaphor in the play. Kay was able to make use of the play, and use metaphor. She told me her sad story over and over in her play/dramas and as long as I was able to stay within the play and help her feel the profound sadness and pain (within my play character) that lay underneath her demeanor of grandiosity, she began to feel accepted and understood. In other words, within the play, I made interpretations of her symptoms that were being played out, that she was able to accept. The working-through element in our work where she played out her life story over and over allowed Kay to develop ego mastery and was insight generating because together we put language to her deeply buried feelings. As her ego developed and she felt more confident in herself she became capable of tolerating and recovering from my empathic failures, which gave her the opportunity to work through traumatic experiences.

Conclusion

I now return to the children's book, *Charlie and the Chocolate Factory* (Dahl, 1964), mentioned at the beginning of this chapter. Kay was very much like the book's pathologically greedy children: Violet Beauregarde, Veruca Salt, Augustus Gloop, and Mike Teavee. All of these fictional children, and the very real Kay, exhibited "features usually described in the past in terms of oral imprints of character, such as impetuosity, imperative demandingness, and insatiability [which] are also related to lack of frustration tolerance, and impulse control and to an inconsistent and unreliable internalization of superego standards and ideals" (Blum, 1991, p. 296). When Kay first began her analysis, it was clear that her aggression destroyed all that was good in all of her objects. Her development of "object constancy" was delayed or we could say she had "hostile object constancy", as she was unable to hold on to the good of the object and had internalized a hateful self-object. As I demonstrated, Kay's analytic treatment helped her to develop new defenses that in turn aided her development so she could reenter the social world and have a better chance for healthier relationships. As I stated earlier, Kay remained somewhat greedy and narcissistic, but like the fictional Charlie, she was now better able to self regulate and hold her greed in check. Kay did not win the prize of a chocolate factory, but she was given a much better chance for a more promising future.

CHAPTER SEVEN

The angry child

The psychoanalytic study of aggression began with the publication of Freud's *Beyond the Pleasure Principle* (1920g), in which he proposed wishes for self-extinction—essentially masochism—to be primary, and outward aggression (sadism) to be a later development. Aggression has a complex and bifurcated history. Early on, Freud (1908c) regarded aggression to be a "component-instinct" of sexuality, a formulation that got elaborated later in his *Instincts and their Vicissitudes* (1915c). Moreover, aggression was seen as a response to the threatened "self-preserving instinct". In these formulations, the sadistic component of aggression was primarily and masochism, if it appeared on the horizon, was "secondary" direction of aggression. These views got turned upside down when later consensus has been that aggression is understood to be an instinctual drive bound for destruction, but not death. Freud described the aggressive drive as destructive, which gave aggression a bad reputation and left many confused about its positive function in psychic development (Downey, 1984). The aggressive drive is a "counterforce to life-sustaining libidinal instincts. Aggression and its apparent drive derivatives are ubiquitous in day-to-day life: and the manifestations of aggression occasion respect and admiration as well as dread and caution in the observer and often the aggressor." (Mayes & Cohen, 1993, p. 146)

Freud's theory of aggression came relatively late, many years after the libidinal drive had secured its' place in the milieu of mental functioning. Freud constructed the aggressive drive to complement the libidinal drive. Early on, years before the structural theory, Freud reasoned that aggressive impulses were included in a drive to master sexual impulses (Freud, 1905d). By 1915, Freud began to conceptualize aggressive impulses as a drive for "mastery or self-preservation and self-nonself differentiation" (Mayes & Cohen, 1993, p. 149). In *Beyond The Pleasure Principle* (1920g), Freud tackled the problem that analysts were seeing in their patients—hostile aggressive actions were not occurring in the service of self-preservation. Patients exhibited self-destructive behavioral patterns, and unrelenting depressions were ubiquitous (Brenner, 1971). Some psychoanalytic scholars speculate that Freud was influenced by the bloodshed of World War I. In addition, Freud suffered the death of his daughter. Many wonder how much this traumatic loss influenced Freud's understanding of aggression (Gay, 1988). Freud did not conceptualize aggression as necessary for normal psychic development. He positioned aggression "outside not only the pleasure principle, but perhaps more importantly, outside the shaping influence of early experience and outside any developmental framework" (Mayes & Cohen, 1993, p. 150). Even though Freud seemed to place less significance on the aggressive drive, his students and followers continued to emphasize the role of aggression in character formation. Some theorists connected infantile oral sadism and toddler-aged anal sadism to later character development, thus grounding their theory in aggression (Abraham, 1923, 1925; Reich, 1933). Others claimed that the aggressive drive serves an important role in object preserving needs as aggression combines with libidinal instincts and is modified (Hartmann et al., 1948. All of these contemporaries of Freud "suggested there were at least three other routes for the modulation of aggression (sublimation, displacement to other objects and restriction of aim) so that aggressive impulses were available for psychic structure formation (superego)" (Mayes & Cohen, 1993, p. 151).

The earliest child analysts such as Kline and Anna Freud, as well as past and current infant researchers agree that aggression is clearly apparent and is essential as the infant separates and develops a differentiated sense of self. Mayes and Cohen state: "aggressivity and aggressive feelings are rooted in the earliest and most basic biologically determined patterns of behavior designed to protect the child and bring others to him in times of need" (Mayes & Cohen, 1993, p. 151). Aggression in the first four years of life is less hostile and destructive then in later years and is thought of by child analysts as a constructive force that fuels object relations. Aggression is essential in helping the young child separate and individuate, and contributes to the development of object constancy. The child requires aggression in order to love and hold those she loves in mind. Aggression is also necessary in shaping the child's developing sense of self (Mahler et al., 1975; Winnicott, 1950). Mayes and Cohen state: "aggression makes it possible for the child to be a separate individual who is capable of identifications, introspections, and partial mergings so characteristic of love relationships. The very separateness fostered and facilitated by the child's early aggressivity allows the child the capacity to be close without losing his hard won, separate sense of self." (Mayes & Cohen, 1993, p. 148)

In the second half of the first year of life, the infant develops object permanence and "an external reality shared with the parent" (Mayes & Cohen, 1993, p. 152). The very young child has developed trust in the primary caregiver and feels safe enough to tolerate hating and loving the mother and begins to integrate these conflicting emotions (Winnicott, 1945, 1969, 1971). At this same time, infants often create a transitional object that is used to alleviate the loss, which accompanies self-differentiation. The transitional object holds magical abilities and fills that transitional space and becomes the first not-me possession. The emergence of a "transitional object signals the knitting together of sexual and aggressive drives in the service of developing safe and stable object relations" (Downey, 1984, p. 113).

Trauma

Very young children who have experienced chronic illness and who have undergone medical procedures because of an illness may interpret these experiences as being hurt by the person or people they depend on the most. Because the child might need to be restrained for medical procedures she is unable to use her body to protect herself and may experience a sense of helplessness. Three- and four-year-old children are still figuring out what is inner and what is outer, what is real and what is fantasy or pretend. Most importantly, they are also experiencing "what it means to hold aggressive wishes and feelings toward those they love and depend upon" (Mayes & Cohen, 1993, p. 165). Child psychoanalysts have been greatly troubled with the effect of early traumatic experiences on the child's inner developing world. When a child meets with unexplainable hurtful experiences, she may begin to view the world as unfriendly, punishing, and frightening.

Solnit tells us that when a young child experiences trauma, his "irritable, aggressive reaction may be his first response of recovery and adaptation" (Solnit, 1970, p. 266). Solnit views aggressivity, in these situations, as a move toward health and a turning away from illness. He states: "aggressive behavior in such instances may be viewed as the return of drive energies available for relating to love objects and life in the external world" (Solnit, 1970, p. 270).

The case of Lizzie

Two weeks after birth, Lizzie stopped defecating. Her parents were told to stimulate her anus with an anal thermometer. This produced bowel movements that looked like *hard sticks*. Breastfeeding was not going well. Lizzie's mother pumped and added her breast milk to formula, and Lizzie was fed by a bottle. The constipation persisted and by three weeks of age the pediatrician examined her anus, told her parents she had a *tiny hinny,* and put her on a daily dose of MiraLax. Lizzie's parents remember her as being extremely uncomfortable pulling her little legs up in pain. The MiraLax caused projectile defecation sometimes hitting the nursery wall four feet away. The dosage was adjusted and by six weeks of age, Lizzie seemed to be fine, no longer in pain, and defecated more or less normally. During these early weeks Lizzie's mother was interviewing all over the country for a prestigious job. Lizzie's father and maternal grandmother took care of Lizzie and her three older brothers. This was a stressful time for Lizzie and her family.

Development

When Lizzie was six months old the family relocated for the mother's job, and around the same time it became clear that Lizzie had upper body low muscle tone. Her gross motor milestones were delayed. She did not sit up unattended until twelve months old and walked at age two; however, cognitively she was advanced with superior verbal skills. The parents did not begin toilet training until after Lizzie's third birthday. This was a conscious decision and a parental value as all of the children began toilet training at age three. A potty was put in front of the television where Lizzie would sit. For several months she neither defecated nor urinated into the potty until one day she stood up and when she saw that she had *pooped three tiny poops into the potty, she decompensated to a state where she could not be comforted until a diaper was put on her.* Lizzie did not defecate for two weeks after this experience and her parents became distraught, worried about an upcoming family vacation. While on this family vacation, Lizzie experienced severe stomach discomfort. When the family arrived at their hotel destination *Lizzie exploded and had feces all over the back of her dress and all over her body, even in her hair.* This pattern persisted where Lizzie would withhold feces for several days and then experience severe discomfort and then a traumatic elimination that would cover her body and her bed. Lizzie's parents stated that Lizzie was extremely unhappy, crying all of the time. This situation curtailed the family's ability to go on outings. This continued for several weeks until one evening Lizzie was in excruciating pain, screaming: *Help me! Help me!* She was given two enemas and more MiraLax that brought no relief. Her parents became so alarmed that they took her to the emergency room. Her parents described this experience as a *nightmare.* They were kept waiting for hours while Lizzie screamed. An x-ray and ultrasound were normal. She was finally admitted into the hospital at four in the morning.

Hospital experience

Lizzie's first hospital stay was traumatic. Her mother or father never left her side as she underwent intrusive medical testing. There were concerns that Lizzie might have spina bifida or a rare degenerative syndrome. Lizzie had to fast, which prevented her from eating over a three-day period. This resulted in her becoming dehydrated, which in turn prolonged her hospital stay. Lizzie's parents described these intrusive medical procedures as a rape. Parents of a hospitalized child who are being told that their child might have a significant illness, are thrust into a counter-intuitive corner as the very treatment that holds hope and promise of a cure, is also the tormentor and abuser of their child. Parents have no choice but to participate in what, to Lizzie's parents, felt like a violent intrusion into their daughter's little three-year-old body; it felt like a rape.

Lizzie's tests were inconclusive and she was sent home with instructions to insert a tube into her rectum every night so that her feces could drain. This continued for a month after which she returned for a second traumatic hospitalization when she was diagnosed with an anal sphincter abnormality. The treatment was Botox injections into her rectum and a recommendation for weekly cognitive behavioral therapy. Her parents were told that she just needed to retrain her body to work normally.

Lizzie's parents followed their doctor's recommendations and Lizzie attended a weekly therapy session with a cognitive behaviorist. Her parents remained very concerned as Lizzie refused to use the potty and it became a battle of wills because the therapist was insisting that Lizzie sit on the potty at regular intervals for a set period of time. Lizzie continued to present as an *unhappy* little girl, who easily fell apart and became inconsolable. Lizzie was also extremely concerned about her body and could not tolerate the tiniest skinned knee and worried about becoming sick. Lizzie did not show any improvement, and in fact seemed to be getting worse as her separation anxiety worsened: she ate very few foods, would not go to birthday parties or on play dates, and at four years old was still in diapers and going to preschool.

Lizzie's parents were in treatment with analysts and both of their analysts recommended that they contact me.

Lizzie's analysis

Lizzie appeared much younger then her four years. A very pretty girl with dark, almost black hair, pale alabaster skin, and large green eyes. She wore a serious, worried expression and carried herself like a toddler; unsure of her body in the space she occupied. Her swollen belly protruded and she wore a diaper. Her father brought her for her first session. She was hesitant, but left her father to come with me into my playroom. She stood silent and still at the threshold for several minutes before deciding to explore the dollhouse. Lizzie meticulously arranged the dollhouse to occupy her family constellation. She positioned the father in the kitchen *making dinner* and the little girl and her brothers on the toilet. The mother was at work. Lizzie turned to look at me and told me that the brothers did not have *potty worries, only the sister and the problem is, she will make her poop in her bed.*

At her third session she scooped sand into little cups in the sandbox in silence. In spite of my efforts to engage her she remained disinterested, turning her face away from me. After ten minutes of what I thought was her avoidance of relating to me, she saw something in a small bottle. Her large green eyes grew wide and her body trembled with excitement.

L: *There is something in there. This is a problem. I don't know how to get it out.*

A: *Oh my! Yes this is a problem; I can see this might be a very big problem.*

L: *It's stinky. It is very stinky.*

A: *There is something very stinky in that bottle and this is a very big problem.*

This conversation continued in this vein; the longer the thing was in the bottle, the stinkier it became and the problem became huge. After ten minutes Lizzie looked at me, still very excited:

L: *Do you have any paper towels in this office?*

A: *Yes I do. There they are on top of that shelf* [and I pointed to the roll of paper towels].

L: *Oh no! That is not enough for this problem. This problem is so big we will need a hundred million trillion paper towels to clean up this mess.*

She dumped out *Mr. Stinky* and told me that we needed a toilet to flush him down. I brought her the miniature toilet from the dollhouse, but Lizzie insisted that we take *Mr. Stinky* out of my office and into the bathroom, where together we flushed him away. On returning to the playroom, Lizzie cooked tons and tons of food and devoured all of it, insisting that I have nothing. *I am so starved! I must have all of this food only for me!*

For many sessions Lizzie found lots of Mr. Stinkys that she insisted we keep in a paper cup high up on a shelf. After getting rid of Mr. Stinky, Lizzie would pretend-eat massive quantities of food and then poop everywhere, especially on me. She laughed with hilarity as I groaned that her poop was in my hair and on my back and even in my eyes.

I was meeting with the parents weekly and they informed me that as soon as Lizzie was put to bed she defecated and then needed to be tended to. Her parents felt that they *walked on eggshells* in order to avoid making her angry and our parent sessions were beneficial in helping them begin to tolerate and help Lizzie with her aggression. Lizzie had a difficult time tolerating disappointment, and would have horrific temper tantrums when she was faced with not getting her way. Her parents went to great lengths to avoid disappointing Lizzie. Within our parent sessions, they began to understand that Lizzie would interpret her parents (and siblings) *walking on eggshells* as not being able to tolerate or accept her difficult aggressive feelings. In addition, this gave Lizzie too much power because she controlled the whole family, and this terrified her.

For the next few weeks, Lizzie's sessions were filled with animals, both toys and imaginary, pooping everywhere, especially all over me! I received a report from her parents that she had successfully defecated into the potty without tears or any apparent fear. After many sessions of this repetitive play she added a new dimension to our sessions. She began to draw girls on the white board with very long tongues. Each girl was a different color and the girls would be erased very quickly, except for their extraordinarily long tongues. As she erased the Orange Girl and the Blue Girl and the Red Girl, I was told to cry because they had left me. Over several weeks the demand that I feel sad and cry when each girl left evolved into Lizzie and myself having angry tantrums because we were left all alone. When I wondered why the girls left, but their tongues remained, Lizzie patiently informed me that *of course they have to leave their tongues! How else will they get food?* Lizzie's sessions over the course of the first few months were exhausting. She worked hard showing me how angry she was as she defecated all over my office and myself. She demonstrated her rage at feeling left and her fear of her own oral greed as she gobbled up all the food or needed a complicated gigantic tongue that was not attached to a body, in order to be fed.

Parent work

At this point I would like to emphasize that my weekly sessions with Lizzie's parents were imperative in the progress and success of her analysis. Both parents were in analytic treatments of their own, were highly intelligent, psychologically minded, and determined to help their daughter. They were willing to explore Lizzie's scary and unpleasant feelings and help her tolerate and modify them. They understood that Lizzie was developmentally regressed and needed intensive treatment to get back on track. In addition, both parents were traumatized by Lizzie's hospital experiences and understood that they needed to work through their own difficult feelings in order to help Lizzie with her trauma. Finally, they understood that Lizzie's symptom of withholding stool was a communication that we needed to listen to. When Lizzie became toilet trained just two months after we began her analysis, they knew we still had much work to do and were completely supportive of her treatment.

Trauma material

Lizzie, now toilet trained, began to catch up developmentally. She had a wonderful summer at her preschool camp as she joined the other children her age in the swimming pool. She brought me her camp backpack and took great joy in emptying it out on my office floor to show me her change of underwear that were decorated in her favorite characters. After a successful family vacation, Lizzie returned to her analysis where trauma material began to emerge. Her parents reported that when she fell and skinned her knee or got a splinter at the playground, she was unable to tolerate the injury to her body and would cry for hours, not able to accept comfort. In her play dramas I became the three-year-old child and she the adult. Many terrible accidents occurred where I was left to cry without comfort, while she, as the adult, received ice cream and candy and all good things. *Mr. Stinky* became defiant and refused to go into the cup. When this happened Lizzie became enraged with me and *quacked* (like a duck) angrily at me, ignoring my efforts to translate her angry and aggressive quacky noises into words. On those days, she left her sessions angry with me. Lizzie told me this was duck language and if I knew anything I would be able to translate without asking. In drama after drama, either I, as her victim, or toy animals met with catastrophes where there was no solution and no repair. In her hairdresser scenario, the little girl was forced to get her hair cut as her mother (Lizzie) screamed: *You have to! You have to!* In her games, body parts became broken or were deformed and there was no *magic medicine* to cure the problems. Lizzie would become frantic as she called for the ambulance, but the ambulance never arrived and the poor child or animal was left to suffer.

Lizzie went back to the whiteboard game where she drew girls of many colors. On this particular day Lizzie drew Red Girl with an extremely defective tongue. Lizzie set up five telephones next to her and called eight ambulances. The ambulances arrived one by one, but Red Girl refused to be helped.

L: *Red Girl won't let anybody help her not even her Mommy. But I love my Mommy! Not even her Daddy! But I love my Daddy! I can't do it. It's too big of a job for me.*

A: *What about me? Would Red Girl let me help?*
L: *No … well, maybe.*

She erased Red Girl except for her enormous defective tongue. After this Lizzie was exhausted and went into my office and lay down on my analytic couch and asked me to read to her.

The treatment deepens

Over the next year Red Girl and Orange Girl and Blue Girl finally went with the ambulance. The play changed to her brothers and herself having a babysitter while her parents went out. The brothers got into big trouble and once again she was powerless in getting the ambulance to come and help. Lizzie continued to express her aggression by pooping in my office and on me, but she also, at times, allowed our characters to accomplish great tasks. We became two circus performers who walked a death-defying tightrope across the length of my office. There was great excitement in our accomplishments and a celebration commenced.

Lizzie entered kindergarten at a new school and adjusted nicely to the more structured environment. She was able to use the bathroom in the classroom, made friends with other children, had play dates, and for the first time was able to go to birthday parties. She also began gymnastic classes and swimming lessons. Lizzie was actually terrified of making mistakes and became extremely rule-bound, sometimes chastising other children for not behaving properly, which, at times, was not appreciated by her classmates. I understood her extreme need to be rule-bound as a compromise formation. Lizzie remained terrified of her own aggression, and like her explosive bowel movements, she was afraid her aggression would become uncontrollable and destroy everyone she cared about and loved.

Within her sessions she continued to combine her newfound abilities, such as accomplished circus performer, with regressive and aggressive pooping play. In addition she developed a new game where a family of snakes (Mommy and babies) lived in my sandbox. In this play the tables were turned and the babies forced the mommy snake to take vile medicine, stuffing sand into the rubber snake until it burst and vomited *all over everybody in the whole world.* I wondered if she had felt like the mommy snake when she was in the hospital. Lizzie responded by telling me about being awake all night and being stuck with needles, and how bad her tummy felt. The next day and for several months she devised a new drama. Lizzie went into my art closet and took out the play dough and made many little girls (in reality they were balls of clay). She then took a box of the tiniest beads, some as small as a pinhead and mushed them into the clay girls. She spent hours *operating* on each girl, extracting the beads. As she did this we spoke about the painful procedures the girls had to endure, how scared they were, and especially how angry they became that their bodies were being intruded into.

Lizzie successfully completed kindergarten, went to a new, more sophisticated summer camp where her brothers also attended, enjoyed a family vacation, and entered first grade ahead of many of her peers academically. Her parents cut down their sessions with me to twice per month and began to take turns. After a few months they began to alternate coming to see me monthly. Lizzie moved away from her trauma themes to her fears about growing up. She used my computer to author a book that she titled *The Angry Baby.* Lizzie's book was quite unusual. She wrote hundreds of pages of random letters that began in the tiniest font and grew larger and larger until one letter almost filled a page. As she did this work, Lizzie narrated and made angry baby cries and screams as the letters grew up until the largest letter was too old to live and had to die. I commented how difficult it is to grow up and no longer be a baby (I added in the good things about growing up also!), and how scared the angry baby was that her mommy and daddy might someday get too old to live.

Separations

After a break due to my vacation, on returning, Lizzie began her session by making a magic potion that removed all of my hair.

L: *Now you are a man, you don't have any hair.*
A: *Oh, so I am bald. I must be a daddy now.*

[Lizzie became worried, pausing for a few minutes and then assured me]

L: *Don't worry, he didn't take your vagina, you are still a girl. You can be a boy and a girl. You can have a penis and a vagina. I'm still a girl. My vagina is safe.*

A: *I can see where a girl could worry about her vagina. If I am bald I might only have a penis and be a boy.*

L: *I think I could have both. It isn't fair to only have one.*

For the next several weeks, Lizzie's body integrity fears were intensified. Scrapes and splinters were catastrophes, and she became extremely fearful of vomiting. Through all of these heightened fears, she continued to work through fears of lost body parts, confusion over gender, and her whiteboard girls with extraordinary tongues returned.

Gradually Lizzie seemed to be more relaxed, and her confidence increased as she invented a new game using all of my analytic journals. She spread the journals all over my office and told me they were lily pads and she was a young girl frog. I, as her frog teacher, made her perform many dangerous and arduous feats so that she could graduate and move to her own pond. After many months of perfecting frog feats and graduating from frog high school, Lizzie moved back into the playroom where princesses went on adventures, met handsome princes, got married, had children, and many family scenarios were played out.

For the most part, Lizzie made excellent progress in her analysis with regressions around my vacations, as she was sure I would not come back. At those times her pooping play reappeared and she would demonstrate how she felt enraged by my leaving her by pooping on me. Now, unlike in the earliest months of her treatment, I could put words to her fear of losing me and how angry and scared my absence made her feel.

Termination

After three years of analysis, Lizzie had caught up developmentally and soared ahead of her age mates. There were some difficulties at home with trying new foods and going to bed at night, but her parents handled these issues very well and they were short-lived. Lizzie's parents were ready for her to terminate with the knowledge and understanding that Lizzie would most probably need to return to treatment around the time of puberty. Lizzie spoke about how she would come back to see me when she was grown and I would be a very old lady and hoped I would not die so she could come back to visit me. Lizzie was also able to verbalize that she was sad to end but at the same time excited because now she could take ballet.

Discussion

"Aggression looms larger than sex in child analysis, dominates the child patients acting out and transference behaviour" (Freud, 1972, p. 168). This was certainly the case in Lizzie's analysis. During the pre-Oedipal years, when the child is in the anal phase of psychosexual development and the rapprochement phase of separation-individuation, feces are a gift from the infant to the mother and by age three "are not supposed to be used aggressively" (Freud, 1972, p. 166). I understand Lizzie's use of aggressive behaviors to be "in the service of the ego, i.e. for the purpose of defense as a reaction to anxiety and a effective cover for it" (Freud, 1972, p. 168). We will never really know the reason why Lizzie withheld her feces to the point of excruciating discomfort and pain. We know that she was born with upper body low muscle tone and had difficulty with elimination while a neonate. We also know that her mother was under tremendous pressure professionally during her pregnancy and for the early months after Lizzie's birth. One of Lizzie's presenting problems was separation anxiety and fear of growing up. All of these complicated early concerns were exacerbated by her hospitalizations and subsequent medically intrusive procedures, which were experienced as traumatic by Lizzie and her parents. I imagine that Lizzie felt helpless and experienced the traumatic hospitalizations as an assault to her fragile ego.

When Lizzie began her analysis she was behind developmentally. Her traumatic experiences had caused a severe regression. Lizzie was socially withdrawn and her play, in her early months of treatment, was constricted. In addition, the trauma had caused an increased arousal where going to bed at night was difficult and she fell apart easily with exaggerated responses to disappointments and normal scrapes and cuts. As noted in her history, Lizzie, at age three, decompensated when she looked into her potty and saw *three little poops*. I speculate that Lizzie was experiencing difficulties as she entered her Oedipal phase and imagined that her three little poops were a part of her body that had broken off. It was this incident that seemed to catapult Lizzie into her cycle of withholding feces for weeks at a time. She had exaggerated bodily fears that were then severely exacerbated by her traumatic hospital stays. Lizzie's play where she makes me into a boy/girl and worries about her own genitals was a valuable part of her analysis where she began to work through castration anxiety and some gender confusion.

Lizzie made excellent use of her analysis as she played out, in her many creative dramas and stories, vicissitudes of aggression where she turned passive experiences into active mastery. Lizzie's aggression manifested as destructive, negative, and at times, hostile, but it seems clear that it also served as a positive force in her psychological growth. When she entered kindergarten and became extremely rule bound she was terrified of making a mistake and would not undertake a new challenge if she thought she might not be successful. These behaviors pointed to a fragile self-esteem as she continued to experience fears of separation. Lizzie's repetitive play was a reflection of her trauma. Where, early in her analysis, she continuously pooped all over my office and myself, and when she drew brightly colored girls with unusual tongues who would not accept help. The tongues had multiple meanings for Lizzie, from oral greed to upward displace of castration anxiety, to the very real experience she endured of a rubber tube inserted into her anus at night. Her play of operating on the clay girls, removing tiny beads with a sharp implement, was another way Lizzie worked through trauma as well as unconscious conflicts.

Lizzie's analysis helped her to modify and begin to find new adaptive resolutions to her conflicts. Many child analysts have written about the importance of displacement as a technique in child analysis (Neubauer, 1993). It was extremely important that I not interfere with Lizzie's need to work through her separation conflicts and her trauma using displacement as evidenced in her many play themes. Lizzie's angry baby and frog games helped lessen her defenses against painful feelings as she or I, played a vulnerable character. As her analysis progressed, Lizzie's fantasy life expanded, and she was able to work through difficult, complex conflicts and destructive feelings. Mayes and Cohen state: "Feelings of neglect or disappointment that for the toddler may have contributed directly to the physical enactments of aggression may now be tempered in the child's fantasy life. Hostile, angry, destructive feelings experienced first with important others may be placed at least temporarily in the security of imaginary play and various solutions to such feelings tried on while the child is safely protected by his loving ties to the same person with whom he is angry." (Mayes & Cohen, 1993, p. 160) However, I did not feel that Lizzie's play was always unconscious and at those times I wondered with her about her hospital experiences and intrusive medical procedures or about her fears of growing up and dying. By the end of her treatment, Lizzie had begun to reflect on her own thoughts and feelings and thus, was better able to understand her angry feelings and put words to them instead of communicating through somatic symptoms or acting out with tantrums.

Conclusion

Lizzie made improvements and got back on track developmentally relatively quickly. I attribute Lizzie's success to several factors: her close positive relationship with both parents; both parents were totally supportive of the treatment and regularly participated in parent sessions; both parents were highly intelligent and psychologically minded realizing that symptom relief did not mean the end of treatment; and lastly, Lizzie was creative and gifted intellectually, which contributed to her resilience. I feel that Lizzie's parents were successful in helping their daughter modify and metabolize the damaging effects of her trauma and were proud of her progress. Very shortly after Lizzie's last session, she sent me a video of herself riding her bicycle without training wheels. A great accomplishment! Over the last couple of years, Lizzie has come back in for visits to tell me about her many adventures and achievements. It is a pleasure for me to see how she has blossomed into a confident and radiant young girl.

Lizzie was extremely lucky as she had parents who came to understand her derailed and regressed development, which resulted in "out-of control" and overwhelming aggression, as a communication for help. Lizzie was experiencing separation anxiety and was unable to modulate her aggressive impulses. In addition, she was dealing with the aftermath of traumatic medical procedures, which threatened her already fragile ego and sense of self. It seemed that Lizzie was unable to tolerate both her hating and her loving feelings toward her parents, which was exacerbated by her confusing experiences of being hurt by the people she loved and depended on. The traumatic hospital experiences were unexplainable to Lizzie and may have been experienced as punishing and most certainly frightening. Three-year-old Lizzie had no other way of communicating her fears of bodily intrusion and of "coming apart". Throughout her three-year analysis, Lizzie was able to metabolize and modify her hostile aggression, which in turn allowed her to begin to separate and individuate. Lizzie continues to flourish.

EPILOGUE

CHAPTER EIGHT

Child analysis—future directions

As described in the beginning of this book, child analysis has a history of suffering from an identity crisis, and now, in the twenty-first century, child analysis is in more than an identity crisis, it is in sharp decline. Analytic institutes internationally and across the United States have a small number of child candidates in training. The past two decades have witnessed a paradigm shift. Parents are often seeking short-term, quick fix treatments. Many parents want their child to be provided with life-skills and given behavioral directions. Cognitive behavioral therapy (CBT) and dialectical behavioral therapy (DBT) have come into favor. Many parents and teachers are misguided and jump to an assumption that a child has ADHD and seek medication as the sole treatment. Health insurance companies often do not reimburse enough for treatment and/or have a high deductible. Young families struggle financially where both parents need to work leaving little time for just being with their children. In addition, children are over-scheduled. They are enrolled in before-and-after-care, and are signed up for numerous assorted after-school extra-curricular activities.

Widening scope

Just as there has been a widening scope in adult psychoanalysis, child analysis too, has seen a widening scope. I believe that healthier (neurotic) children, do very well in a twice per week psychoanalytic psychotherapy. However, in a perfect world where time and finances are abundant, the healthier, neurotic child would benefit greatly from an analytic treatment. Since this is not the case for most families, a psychoanalytic psychotherapy with parent involvement in the treatment can often get children back on track developmentally within a year or two and treatment can then end. Child analysts are confronted with and treat children who face difficult obstacles to healthy development such as autism, blindness, and deafness. In addition, children who have experienced trauma—such as Georgie, who spent his first ten months in an orphanage lying on his back staring at the ceiling; Kay, who witnessed domestic violence, and was physically hurt and neglected by her mother when an infant; Sara, who spent her first two years of life living on the street with her mother who was cognitively limited and had difficulty mothering; Bella, whose mother slept through her childhood obviously extremely depressed and narcissistic; Helen, who was born with autism and whose parents were unable to provide the appropriate treatment; and Lizzie who experienced trauma at the hands of her medical doctors—all need intensive analytic treatments in order to progress and get back on track developmentally. Solnit states: "there is no absolute psychoanalytic technique for use with children, but rather a set of analytic principles which have to be adapted to specific cases" (Solnit, 2001, p. 8). This is especially true in our current environment. It is important to remember that Anna Freud learned much about loss and attachment during the war and applied what she learned to her theory and technique of child analysis. From this important work she was able to make inferences about how early deprivation adversely affects normal development. Anna Freud was influential in widening the scope by treating delinquent adolescents who previously were considered unsuitable for psychoanalysis. In addition, in Vienna, in the Edith Jackson nursery, Anna Freud and her colleagues treated the poorest families and even the homeless. In the 1950s, Anna Freud reached out further into the community. This "included observations in the baby clinic, toddler group, nursery school, and a school for the blind" (Colonna, 2001, p. 12). However, she counseled child analysts to value neurotic disorders and to focus on the infantile neurosis. She urged child analysts to concentrate on the transference, resistance, and interpreting the defenses (Abrams, 2001). Like Solnit, Anna Freud individualized her treatments to fit the case, including the use of parent education. In her view, technique "was a way of thinking and applying theoretical principles" (Colonna, 2001, p. 11). For Anna Freud, the goal of child analysis is to help the child regain normal development. For example, I stated that Kay terminated her analysis because she was developmentally age-appropriate. Kay's analysis demonstrates how through her many play scenarios, she remembered, reconstructed, and reenacted her painful past. In our enactments, where I disappointed her, or where she felt betrayed by me, healing began, and she allowed herself to trust that we could repair our ruptures and regain our footing.

While Anna Freud and her followers were progressive for their time, they focused on the psychic structures, with emphasis on the ego and analysis of defenses. Mahler's work, based on empirical observational data, centers on separation-individuation. Mahler's theory implies a biological momentum as the child moves from symbiosis to hatching to autonomy, but observers stress that problems in development result from the interaction between the mother and child. For many years the developmental theories of both Anna Freud and Mahler were condemned as anti-analytic (Abrams, 2001).

In recent years child analysis has experienced a shift from the intrapsychic to the intersubjective. With the work of infant researchers such as Beebe and Tronick, as well as the work of the Boston Process of Change Study Group (BPCSG), the focus has shifted toward object relations and intersubjectivity. BPCSG argues that interpretation is not enough for change to occur. It states: "more resides in interactional intersubjective processes that give rise to implicit relational knowing" (Stern et al., 1998, p. 903). BPCSG bases its theory on infant-mother interaction, proposing that there are special "moments of authentic person-to-person connection with the therapist that alter the relationship with him and thereby the patients' sense of himself" (Stern et al., 1998, p. 913).

Working with parents

Hug-Hellmuth, in her paper *On the Technique of Child Analysis* (1921), clearly states that parents often feel that psychoanalysis is a last resort, and enter into the treatment full of shame, feeling they have failed their child. The parents yearn for a relationship with the analyst. Hug-Hellmuth feels the parents' desire to interact with their child's analyst is "a legitimate demand on the part of the parents" (Hug-Hellmuth, 1921, p. 304). She proposed, in 1921, that it is extremely beneficial to work with the parents within the transference. Klein, on the other hand, rarely spoke with parents. Klein felt that her job with parents was to keep them from interfering with the child's treatment. Anna Freud's relationship with parents was educative, giving advice about child development and behaviors (Plastow, 2015). Both Anna Freud and Klein set the example of working exclusively with the child in an analysis (Novick & Novick, 2005). In the 1960s through the 1980s in the United States, it was customary for an analyst to see the child, while simultaneously the parents were sent to a social worker. In this way the parents were kept out of the analysis. In the 1990s and early 2000s, child candidates were taught to meet with the parents occasionally and refer them for their own analysis. This is still a viable and often favorable option, but for some families not possible for a variety of reasons.

Just as Winnicott stated that there is no such thing as a baby without a mother, there is also no such thing as a child analysis without a positive working relationship with the parents. There are several objectives to working with the parents. First and foremost, a therapeutic alliance must be built and maintained with the parents for the analysis to be successful. This is essential in order to maintain the treatment during difficult periods of the analysis. I always meet with parents for several sessions before evaluating their child. Within these parent sessions I make sure that the parents understand that their child's treatment is a group effort, we are all working together to help the child. When the parents are on board and maintain a committed working relationship with the analyst, the child understands that the parents and analyst are working together for the benefit of the child. If jealousies arise, as they did in Georgie's analysis, the child often feels he is betraying the parent by choosing to be with the analyst. The child is put in the middle and may feel a conflict of loyalty. In the case of Georgie, the negative transference that the father developed toward me was never resolved and caused the analysis to end prematurely. This is a case where the father would have benefited greatly from his own treatment. I still regret that I was unable to convince him to enter into his own treatment.

Work with parents within the analytic treatment of children has evolved over the past two decades. Plastow elaborates on the parent's sense of shame and feelings of failure, stressing that failure is also experienced as guilt that is often ignored and left unspoken. This unspoken sense of guilt and shame can fester and further damage the child's relationship with her parent and/or destroy the treatment (Plastow, 2015). Perhaps most helpful, working with the parents "involves reducing the guilt feelings and fears of failure that assail parents" (Holder, 2005, p. 105). Novick and Novick, in their innovative book *Working with parents makes therapy work* (2005), echo Hug-Hellmuth when they state that when parents arrive in our treatment rooms they have often exhausted other therapies and are desperate for results and often demand that the analyst "fix" their "broken" child. In addition, when child analysts write about and present child analytic cases, the work with parents is, for the most part, not included. This gives the impression that the parents remain outside the treatment and are unimportant.

Looking back to the beginnings of child analysis, as stated in the beginning of this book, the first child analysis was conducted via the parent by Freud (1909b). A shift occurred to focusing on the internal world of the child as Freud developed his developmental psychosexual phases, which were understood to be independent of the environment. This shift in theory validated "ignoring the role of the parents in the treatment of children" (Novick & Novick, 2005, p. 3). There is much to say about including parents in the child's treatment and the Novicks have written extensively on this subject. I wish to emphasize, in agreement with the Novicks, that most child analysts realize that there cannot be a successful analysis without parent involvement. The Novicks ask child analysts to explore their own resistance and come to terms with their counter-transferences to the parents. They state: "we are often unaware in ourselves of defensiveness, avoidance, awkwardness, procrastination, and so forth in trying to implement our own model" (Novick & Novick, 2005, p. 14). Along these same lines of thinking, Erna Furman (1995) wrote: "When we disregard the parent, we leave out crucial parts of the child's self, sometimes the best parts, and when we treat the parent and disregard the child, we commit the same mistake." (Furman, 1995, p. 27) Lastly, through their intensive research, Fonagy and Target have concluded that the future of child analysis needs to include the whole family, not just the designated child (Fonagy & Target, 2002).

Early in my analytic career, I saw the parents infrequently and referred them to colleagues for their own treatments. Over time and through experience, (for example, my troubled relationship with

Georgie's father), I came to the realization that the parents are a crucial part of the treatment. I feel Lizzie's analysis was successful because of my work with her parents and the feeling that we were working together to get Lizzie back on track developmentally, and my work with Kay's grandparents was imperative to the success of her treatment.

Future research

Peter Fonagy and Mary Target state that there is a dearth of outcome information on child psychoanalytic treatments, which, they feel, is directly related to the research traditions of the Anna Freud Centre. Fonagy and Target conducted a follow up study of adults who were treated when they were children at the Anna Freud Centre. They concluded that regarding "children with emotional disorders, there was evidence that severe or complex symptomatology responded well to intensive treatment, but not to non-intensive treatment" (Fonagy & Target, 2002, p. 33). It is interesting to note that Anna Freud felt that psychoanalysis could be of help for current difficulties the child was experiencing but would not protect the child from later pathology. In contrast to Anna Freud, Fonagy and Target suggest that "psychoanalytic therapy might enhance resilience in the face of later events, enabling the child to understand, predict, and plan for his own and others' responses, particularly within relationships, through, for instance, the capacity for mentalization, a reflection on mental states, enhancing the security and autonomy of internal working models of attachment relationships" (Fonagy & Target, 2002, p. 46). Fonagy and Target state that psychoanalytic treatment changes ego functions and enhances resilience.

Fonagy cautions that CBT should not be the one and only treatment for mental disorders and "that premature commitment to one approach could seriously erode the skill of practitioners" (Fonagy, 2003, p. 129). He further stresses that symptom relief is not an adequate indicator "in relation to the complex interpersonal processes that evolve over hundreds of sessions" (Fonagy, 2003, p. 130). Fonagy states evidence from adult research that directly relates to child treatments: long-term therapy is more effective than short-term therapy; many of the benefits of psychoanalytic treatment seem to emerge after termination (sleeper effect); and intensity matters—the number of sessions per week appears to make a difference (Fonagy, 2003, p. 131). In this research-oriented world, it seems that the field of psychoanalysis needs to conduct more research demonstrating the efficacy of the treatment. Fonagy urges us to determine the specific individuals who best benefit from psychoanalysis and develop an assessment tool to identify these patients. In addition, he recommends that a sensitive measurement be devised that shows changes that go beyond symptom relief. Finally, Fonagy states that child psychoanalysis should evolve and adapt to include more work with parents and families (Fonagy, 2003).

Final thoughts

Exploring the history of child analysis exposes the difficulties that the field of psychoanalysis as a whole has been plagued with for over a century. New concepts and theories are often met with dread and fear that all that came before will be destroyed. Of course in reality this is far from the truth, when in fact, new theory and concepts serve to strengthen our field. It is enlightening to note that while Anna Freud and Klein fought bitterly over their differences in theory and technique, in the twenty-first century child analysts, for the most part, incorporate theory and technique from both of these pioneers. For example, I cannot imagine a child treatment that does not make use of play. Klein stated that play for children is the same as associations are for adults, a way into the child's unconscious wishes and conflicts. We know that play is much more than free associations and more than a path into the unconscious. Play "rests on the ability to displace conflict from primary objects to toys, animals, friends, to search for the resolution of conflicts in relationships with others rather than with primary objects, for these conflicts are too painful to face" (Neubauer, 2001, p. 24). In a therapeutic situation it is through the use of play that a child communicates his inner world to the therapist. The "play state" consists of two interconnecting mechanisms: a psychical component consisting of conscious and unconscious fantasies and wishes, and a physical or acting-out component (Neubauer, 1987). The mental component in play exists between primary and secondary process thinking which allows thinking and doing to merge together.

In order to play, the child must be able to understand internal mental states in the "self" and in others. Fonagy calls this mentalization. Fonagy states that without the ability to mentalize the child is unable to make sense of his world. The child is unable to "find himself in the other as a mentalizing individual" (Fonagy, 1995, p. 257). Fonagy urges clinicians to make use of the play state to facilitate the child's ability to mentalize. Play allows the therapist a "window into the operations of the child's mental functioning and self representations" (Solnit, Cohen, & Neubauer, 1993, p. 2), and by helping the child to be playful and use his imagination, the therapist helps the child to view his own inner world. It is this creative process that is so essential to the development of a self.

Freud stated that the compulsion to repeat is a driving force as the child uses play to gain mastery over developmental conflicts. Freud tells us that the pleasurable feelings are recaptured in play and drive the child to replay events in his life. However, children also make use of play to work through or gain mastery over traumatic and unpleasurable events. The child is able to do this by turning passive into active and gaining a sense of control over powerful experiences in which he had no control. In play, children combine fantasy with reality. Many issues that are too threatening to deal with directly are accepted in play by both the child and the adult (Ritvo, 1993). Playing facilitates creativity, "and it is only in being creative that the individual discovers the self" (Winnicott, 1971, p. 54). The therapeutic relationship becomes the "potential space" in which the child will learn to trust and connect, to be played with and to feel playful. The use of play in this safe space facilitates the child's capacity for reflective thinking as emotions and feelings begin to be categorized, labeled, and given meaning.

As demonstrated by the analytic treatments of the six children in this book, I utilized several different techniques and interventions depending on the individual child's needs. For example, Kay's analysis was conducted almost entirely in the play as she made use of displacement to work through her fears, wishes, and conflicts. On occasion, when I left our transitional safe play space, my interpretations either caused her to shut down or I inflicted a narcissistic wound. For Kay, staying within the domain of play was essential. Lizzie, on the other hand, had a much stronger ego and was able to tolerate and make use of my interpretations both within the play and out of the play, especially as her analysis progressed. With Sara, I needed to put words to her feelings so that she could begin to understand her mind and engage in a relationship with another person. Her trauma was so severe; it took many months before she was able to play.

All six of the children represented in this book demonstrate the value and necessity for intensive psychoanalytic treatment. The current training requirement for candidates, as dictated by our national organization, demands that children be seen for four or five sessions per week. As I stated at the beginning of this chapter, there are many reasons parents are unwilling and/or unable to make this time and financial commitment. For some children, there are no other substitute treatments. I argue that change needs to occur in order to make child psychoanalysis accessible to a greater number of families. First, I encourage the Committee On Child Analysis to reduce the time requirement to three sessions per week. Since families are better able to bring a child three times per week as opposed to four or five, more clinicians will be willing to undertake child analytic training. We cannot expect individuals to make a costly investment in training if the patients are unavailable. Second, we need to demonstrate to our government and to insurance companies, that this treatment is actually cost effective, and needs to be supported. For example, as a benefit to this intensive deep treatment, hospitalizations can be prevented and symptoms such as anorexia and obesity can also be prevented, as well as ending intergenerational transmission of trauma, which affects children in silent yet insidious ways.

Psychoanalytic treatments also serve to preserve the family by supporting interactions. The institution of "family" has changed dramatically and "family time" is rapidly diminishing. Children and parents are often seen together, but focused on their smartphones or iPads, hardly interacting at all, except to fight over who gets the most screen time. It is not unusual to see a young mother pushing her baby in a stroller, talking or texting on her cell phone. Gone are the days of pointing out flowers, and kittens, and birds as mother and baby go on an outing. In addition, our children are being brought up in an extremely competitive environment. Children as young as seven or eight are enrolled in dance teams, swim teams, and soccer teams where they practice four-six times per week and participate in competitions. There is a fear that if your child is not enrolled in several after-school activities, he will be at a great disadvantage and will lose the competitive edge needed to be admitted into the Ivy League college of his choice. What psychoanalysis has to offer is more important than competitive productivity and getting admitted into the perfect pre-school, private school, and college. We need to challenge the current paradigm and demonstrate the value of family interactions on a deeper emotional level. It seems that our modern world has interfered with the meat and potatoes of the closeness and intimacy of relationships.

By the time parents bring their child to my office, the child has behaved in ways that disrupt the family and worry the parents. The child's behaviors are communicating *I need something I am not getting* and the child is in significant emotional pain. Psychoanalysts are trained to work with the family to help discover what that "something missing" is. Along this journey, parents and child begin to understand their own and each other's minds, interactions change, and symptoms disappear, and the ego is strengthened. I hope that sharing my analytic experiences with the six children in this book adequately demonstrates the value of child analytic training, and child psychoanalysis, but also makes clear that we have a huge challenge ahead to help make this treatment more accessible to the masses, not just to the elite few.

NOTE

Chapter Five

1. *Oedipal victor*: The child who seemingly wins the affections of the same-sex parent away from the other parent in fantasy or reality. "This is seen as a tragedy, as it was in the tragedy of Sophocles' *Oedipus Rex*. The tragedy is seen in the consequent disturbances in sexual function and object choice, inhibitions in achievement of any sort, and incomplete coalescence and consolidation of the superego." (Auchincloss & Samberg, 2012, p. 182).

REFERENCES

Abend, S. M. (1988). Intrapsychic versus interpersonal: the wrong dilemma. *Psychoanalytic Inquiry, 8*: 497–504.

Abelin, E. (1971). The role of the father in the separation-individuation process. In: J. B. McDevitt & C. F. Settlage (Eds.), *Separation-Individuation* (pp. 229–252). New York: International Universities Press.

Abraham, K. (1923). Contributions to the theory of the anal character. *International Journal of Psychoanalysis, 4*: 400–418.

Abraham, K. (1925). Influence of oral erotism on character formation. *International Journal of Psychoanalysis, 6*: 247–258.

Abrams, S. (2001). Summation unrealized possibilities comments on Anna Freud's normality and pathology in childhood. *Psychoanalytic Study of the Child, 56*: 105–119.

Akhtar, S. (1992). Tethers, orbits, and invisible fences: clinical, developmental, sociocultural, and technical aspects of optimal distance. In: S. Kramer & S. Akhtar (Eds.), *When the Body Speaks: Psychological Meanings bend in Kinetic Clues* (pp. 21–57). Northvale, NJ: Aronson.

Akhtar, S. (1994). Object constancy and adult psychopathology. *The International Journal of Psychoanalysis, 75*: 441–455.

Akhtar, S. (2009). *Comprehensive Dictionary of Psychoanalysis*. London: Karnac.

149

Akhtar, S., & Powell, A. (2004). Celluloid fathers: the depiction of parental function in some recent movies. In: S. Akhtar & H. Parens (Eds.), *Real and Imaginary Fathers* (pp. 73–94). London: Aronson.

Allured, E. (2006). Developing the intersubjective playground in the treatment of childhood Asperger's syndrome. *Journal of Infant, Child & Adolescent Psychotherapy, 5*: 397–419.

Asperger, H. (1944). Autistic psychopathy in childhood. In: U. Frith (Ed.), *Autism and Asperger Syndrome* (pp. 37–92). New York: Cambridge University Press.

Atwood, T. (2007). *The Complete Guide to Asperger's Syndrome.* Philadelphia, PA: Jessica Kingsley.

Barnett, M. C. (1966). Vaginal awareness in the infancy and childhood of girls. *Journal of American Psychoanalytic Association, 14*: 129–140.

Beebe, B., Lachmann, F., & Jaffe, J. (1997). Mother-infant interaction structures and presymbolic self and object representations. *Psychoanalytic Dialogues, 7*: 133–182.

Benedek, T. (1970). Fatherhood and parenthood. In: E. J. Anthony & T. Benedek (Eds.), *Parenthood: Its Psychology and Psychopathology* (pp. 169–183). Boston, MA: Little, Brown.

Benjamin, J. (1991). Fathers and daughters: identification with difference. *Psychoanalytic Dialogues, 1*: 277–300.

Bergman, A. (2000). Merging and emerging: separation-individuation theory and the treatment of children and disorders of the sense of self. *Journal of Infant, Child & Adolescent Psychotherapy, 1*: 61–75.

Bergman, A., & Escalona, S. K. (1949). Unusual sensitivities in very young children. *Psychoanalytic Study of the Child, 3*: 333–352.

Blum, H. P. (1973). The concept of erotized transference. *Journal of the American Psychoanalytic Association, 21*: 61–76.

Blum, H. P. (1981). Object inconstancy and paranoid reconstruction. *Journal of the American Psychoanalytic, 29*: 789–813.

Blum, H. P. (1991). Dyadic psychopathology and infantile eating disorder psychoanalytic study and inferences. In: S. Akhtar & H. Parens (Eds.), *Beyond the Symbiotic Orbit Advances in Separation-Individuation Theory* (pp. 285–298). Hillsdale, NJ: Analytic.

Blum, H. P. (2008). A further excavation of seduction, seduction trauma, and the seduction theory. *Psychoanalytic Study of the Child, 63*: 254–269.

Boris, H. N. (1976). On hope: its nature and psychotherapy. *The International Review of Psycho-Analysis, 3*: 139–150.

Boris, H. N. (1986). The "other" breast-greed, envy, spite, and revenge. *Contemporary Psychoanalysis, 22*: 45–59.

Bowlby, J. (1960). Grief and mourning in infancy and early childhood. *Psychoanalytic Study of the Child, 15*: 9–52.

Bowlby, J. (1988). *A Secure Base: Parent-Child Attachment and Healthy Human Development*. New York: Basic.

Brenner, C. (1971). The psychoanalytic concept of aggression. *The International Journal of Psychoanalysis, 52*: 137–144.

Bromfield, R. (1989). Psychodynamic play therapy with a high-functioning autistic child. *Psychoanalytic Psychology, 6*: 439–453.

Bromfield, R. (2000). It's the tortoise race: long-term psychodynamic psychotherapy with a high-functioning autistic adolescent. *Psychoanalytic Inquiry, 20*: 732–745.

Chasseguet-Smirgel, J. (1970). Female guilt and the Oedipus complex. In: J. Chasseguet-Smirgel (Ed.), *Female Sexuality: New Psychoanalytic Views* (pp. 94–134). Ann Arbor, MI: University of Michigan Press.

Chodorow, N. (1978). *The Reproduction of Mothering*. Berkeley, CA: University of California.

Coates, S. W. (1998). Having a mind of one's own and holding the other in mind. Commentary on paper by P. Fonagy & M. Target. *Psychoanalytic Dialogues, 8*: 115–148.

Cohler, B. J., & Weiner, T. (2011). The inner fortress: symptom and meaning in Asperger's syndrome. *Psychoanalytic Inquiry, 31*: 208–221.

Colarusso, C. A. (2011). *The Long Shadow of Sexual Abuse: Developmental Effects Across the Life Cycle*. Northvale, NJ: Aronson.

Colonna, A. B. (2001). Opening of discussion. *Psychoanalytic Study of the Child, 56*: 9–15.

Courchesne, E., Carper, R., & Akshoomoof, N. (2003). Evidence of brain overgrowth in the first year of life in autism. *Journal of the American Medical Association, 290*: 337–344.

Davies, J. M. (2003). Falling in love with love: Oedipal and post-Oedipal manifestations of idealization, mourning, and erotic masochism. *Psychoanalytic Dialogues, 13*: 1–27.

Dinnerstein, D. (1976). *The Mermaid and the Minotaur*. New York: Harper & Row.

Downey, T. W. (1984). Within the pleasure principle child analytic perspectives on aggression. *Psychoanalytic Study of the Child, 39*: 101–136.

Eagle, M. (1995). The developmental perspectives of attachment and psychoanalytic theory. In: S. Goldberg, R. Muir, & J. Kerr (Eds.), *Attachment theory social, developmental, and clinical perspectives* (pp. 123–150). Hillsdale, NJ: Analytic.

Emde, R. N. (1981). Changing models of infancy and the nature of early development: remodeling the foundation. *Journal of the American Psychoanalytic Association, 29*: 179–219.

Erikson, E. (1950). *Childhood and Society*. New York: Norton.

Ewens, T. (1976). Female sexuality and the role of the phallus. *The Psychoanalytic Review, 63*: 615–637.

Fenichel, O. (1931). Specific Forms of the Oedipus Complex. In: *The Collected Papers of Otto Fenichel, First Series* (pp. 204–220). New York: Norton, 1954.

Folstein, S. S., & Santangelo, S. L. (2000). Does asperger's syndrome aggregate in families? In: A. Klin, F. R. Volkmar, & S. S. Sparrow (Eds.). *Asperger's Syndrome* (pp. 159–171). New York: Guilford.

Fonagy, P. (1995). Playing with reality: the development of psychic reality and its malfunction in borderline patients. *The International Journal of Psychoanalysis, 76*: 39–44.

Fonagy, P. (2003). The research agenda: The vital need for empirical research in child psychotherapy. *Journal of Child Psychotherapy, 29*: 129–136.

Fonagy, P. (2008). The mentalization-focused approach to social development. In: F. N. Busch (Ed.), *Mentalization: Theoretic Concerns, Research Findings, and Clinical Implications* (pp. 3–56). New York: Analytic.

Fonagy, P., & Target, M. (2002). The history and current status of outcome research at the Anna Freud center. *Psychoanalytic Study of the Child, 67*: 27–60.

Fonagy, P., & Target, M. (1998). Mentalization and the changing aims of child psychoanalysis. *Psychoanalytic Dialogues, 8*: 87–114.

Fraiberg, S. (1982). Pathological defenses in infancy. *Psychoanalytic Quarterly, LI*: 612–635.

Fraiberg, S., Adelson, E., & Shapiro, V. (1975). Ghosts in the nursery: a psychoanalytic approach to the problem of impaired infant-mother relationships. *Journal of the American Academy of Child Psychiatry, 14*(3): 387–421.

Freud, A. (1927). Four Lectures on Child Psychoanalysis. *The Writings of Anna Freud, Volume 1* (pp. 3–62). New York: International Universities Press.

Freud, A. (1936). The ego and the mechanisms of defense. *The Writings of Anna Freud, Volume 2*. New York: International Universities Press, 1966.

Freud, A. (1965). *Normality and Pathology in Childhood*. New York: International Universities Press.

Freud, A. (1970). The infantile neurosis: genetic and dynamic consideration. *The Writings of Anna Freud, Volume 7* (pp. 189–203).

Freud, A. (1972). Comments on aggression. *International Journal of Psychoanalysis, 53*: 163–171.

Freud, A. (1980). Foreword to "Analysis of a Phobia in a Five-year-old Boy". *The Writings of Anna Freud, Volume 8* (pp. 277–282).

Freud, S. (1895d). *Studies on Hysteria. S. E., 2*. London: Hogarth.

Freud, S. (1896c). The Aetiology of Hysteria. *S. E., 3*: 189. London: Hogarth.

Freud, S. (1905d). *Three Essays on the Theory of Sexuality. S. E., 7*: 125. London: Hogarth.

Freud, S. (1908c). On the Sexual Theories of Children. *S. E., 9*: 207. London: Hogarth.

Freud, S. (1909b). Analysis of a Phobia in a Five-Year-Old Boy. *S. E., 10*: 3. London: Hogarth.

Freud, S. (1915c). Instincts and their Vicissitudes. *S. E., 14*: 111. London: Hogarth.

Freud, S. (1917e). Mourning and Melancholia. *S. E., 14*: 239. London: Hogarth.

Freud, S. (1920g). *Beyond the Pleasure Principle. S. E., 18*: 7. London: Hogarth.

Freud, S. (1924d). The Dissolution of the Oedipus Complex. *S. E., 19*: 173. London: Hogarth.

Freud, S. (1930a). *Civilization and its discontents. S. E., 21*: 59. London: Hogarth.

Freud, S. (1940a). *An Outline of Psycho-Analysis. S. E., 23*: 141. London: Hogarth.

Frith, U. (1991). *Autism and Asperger's Syndrome.* Cambridge: Cambridge University Press.

Frith, U. (2004). Confusions and controversies about Asperger's syndrome. *Journal Child Psychology and Psychiatry, 45*: 672–686.

Furman, E. (1995). Working with and through the parents. *Child Analysis, 6*: 21–42.

Gartner, R. B. (Ed.) (1997). *Daring to Remember. A Review of Memories of Sexual Betrayal: Truth, Fantasy, Depression, and Dissociation.* Northvale, NJ: Aronson.

Gay, P. (1988). *Freud.* New York: Norton.

Geissman, C., & Geissman, P. (1992). *A History of Child Psychoanalysis.* London: Routledge.

Ginsburg, L. M. (2003). An unexamined "post-script" to the demise of Sigmund Freud's seduction theory: a spurious reification or prescient second thoughts? *International Forum of Psychoanalysis, 12*: 265–272.

Gill, H. S. (1987). Effects of Oedipal triumph caused by collapse or death of the rival parent. *The International Journal of Psychoanalysis, 68*: 251–260.

Gillberg, C., & Ehlers, S. (1998). High-functioning people with autism and Asperger's syndrome: A literature review. In: E. Schopler, G. B. Mesibov, & L. K. Kunce (Eds.), *Asperger Syndrome or High-Functioning Autism?* (pp. 79–106). New York: Plenum.

Greenacre, P. (1956). Re-evaluation of the process of working through. *International Journal of Psychoanalysis, 23*: 439–444.

Greenspan, S. (1981). *Psychopathology and Adaptation in Infancy and Early Childhood. Principles of Clinical Diagnosis and Preventive Intervention.* New York: International Universities Press.

Greenspan, S. (1990). Comprehensive clinical approaches to infants and families. In: S. Meisels & J. Shonkoff (Eds.), *Handbook of Early Interventions* (pp. 150–72). New York: Cambridge University Press.

Grossman, W. I., & Stewart, W. A. (1976). Penis envy: from childhood wish to developmental metaphor. *Journal of the American Psychoanalytic Association, 24s*: 193–212.

Harrison, A. M. (2005). Herding the animals into the barn: A parent consultation model. *Psychoanalytic Study of the Child, 60*: 128–153.

Harrison, A. M., & Tronick, E. Z. (2011). "The noise monitor": A developmental perspective on verbal and nonverbal meaning-making in psychoanalysis. *Journal of the American Psychoanalytic Association, 59*(5): 961–982.

Hartmann, H. (1948). Comments on the psychoanalytic theories of instinctual drives. *Psychoanalytic Quarterly, 17*: 368–388.

Herzog, J. M. (2004). Father hunger and narcissistic deformation. *Psychoanalytic Quarterly, 73*: 893–914.

Herzog, J. M. (2005). Triadic reality and the capacity to love. *Psychoanalytic Quarterly, 74*: 1029–1052.

Hodges, S. (2004). A psychological perspective on theories of Asperger's syndrome. In: M. Rhode & T. Klauber (Eds.), *The Many Faces of Asperger's Syndrome* (pp. 39–53). New York: Karnac.

Holder, A. (2005). *Anna Freud, Melanie Klein, and the Psychoanalysis of Children and Adolescents*. London: Karnac.

Holmes, J. (2011). Superego: an attachment perspective. *The International Journal of Psychoanalysis, 92*: 1221–1240.

Horney, K. (1924). On the genesis of the castration complex in women. *International Journal of Psychoanalysis, 5*: 50–65.

Horney, K. (1926). The flight from womanhood. In: H. Kelman (Ed.), *Feminine Psychology* (pp. 54–70). New York: Norton.

Hug-Hellmuth, H. (1921). On the technique of child analysis. *International Journal of Psychoanalysis, 2*: 287–305.

Hughes, D. A. (1997). *Facilitating developmental attachment*. Northvale, NJ: Aronson.

Jones, E. (1927). The early development of female sexuality. *International Journal of Psychoanalysis, 8*: 459–472.

Jones, E. (1935). Early female sexuality. *International Journal of Psychoanalysis, 16*: 263–273.

Josephs, L. (2001). The seductive superego: the trauma of self-betrayal. *International Journal of Psychoanalysis, 82*: 701–712.

Kanner, L. (1943). Autistic disturbances of affective contact. *Nervous Child, 2*: 217–250.

Karen, R. (1998). *Becoming Attached: First Relationships and How They Shape Our Capacity to Love*. New York: Warner.

Kieffer, C. C. (2004). Self objects, Oedipal objects, and mutual recognition: a self-psychological reappraisal of the female "Oedipal victor". *The Annual of Psychoanalysis, 32*: 69–80.

Klein, M. (1952). The mutual influences in the development of ego and the id. In: *Envy and Gratitude and Other Works 1946–1963*. New York: Free Press, 1975.

King, R. A. (1993). Cookies for the emperor: The multiple functions of play in the analysis of an early adolescent boy. In: A. J. Solnit, D. J. Cohen, & P. B. Neubauer (Eds.), *The many meanings of play: A psychoanalytic perspective* (pp. 135–154). New Haven, CT: Yale University Press.

Klin, A., McPartland, J., & Volkmar, F. R. (2005). Asperger syndrome. In: F. R. Volkmar, R. Paul, A. Klin, & D. Cohen (Eds.), *Handbook of Autism and Pervasive Developmental Disorders, Volume 1: Diagnosis, Development, Neurobiology, and Behavior* (pp. 88–125). New York: Wiley.

Kohut, H. (1971). *The Analysis of the Self*. New York: International Universities Press.

Kohut, H. (1996). *The Chicago Institute Lectures*. M. Tolpin & P. Tolpin (Eds.). Hillsdale, NJ: Analytic.

Kramer, S., & Akhtar, S. (Eds.) (1991). *The Trauma of Transgression*. Northvale, NJ: Aronson.

Lerner, H. E. (1976). Parental mislabeling of female genitals as a determinant of penis envy and learning inhibitions in women. *Journal of the American Psychoanalytic Association, 24S*: 269–283.

Lincoln, A. E., Courchesne, E., Allen, M., Hanson, E., & Fine, M. (1998). Neurobiology of Asperger's syndrome: Seven case studies and quantitative magnetic resonance imaging findings. In: I. E. Schopler, G. B. Mesibov, & L. J. Kunde (Eds.), *Asperger Syndrome or High-Functioning Autism?* (pp. 145–163). New York: Plenum.

Loewald, H. (1951). Ego and reality. *International Journal of Psychoanalysis, 32*: 10–18.

Loewald, H. (1979). The waning of the Oedipus complex. In: *The Essential Loewald Collected Papers and Monographs* (pp. 384–404). Hagerstown, MD: University Publishing Group, 2000.

Lussier, A. (1999). The dead mother: variations on a theme. In: G. Kohon (Ed.), *The Dead Mother* (pp. 149–162). London: Routledge.

Mahler, M. S., & Gosliner, B. J. (1955). On symbiotic child psychosis: genetic, dynamic, and restitutive aspects. *The Psychoanalytic Study of the Child, 10*: 195–212.

Mahler, M. S., Pine, F., & Bergman, A. (1975). *The Psychological Birth of the Human Infant: Symbiosis and Individuation*. New York: Basic.

Mahler, M. S. (1952). On child psychosis and schizophrenia—autistic and symbiotic infantile psychoses. *The Psychoanalytic Study of the Child, 7*: 286–305.

Mahler, M. S. (1961). On sadness and grief in infancy and childhood—loss and restoration of the symbiotic love object. *The Psychoanalytic Study of the Child, 16*: 332–351.

Mahler, M. S. (1963). Thoughts about development and individuation. *The Psychoanalytic Study of the Child, 18*: 307–324.

Mahler, M. S. (1967). Discussion of "Problems of over-idealization of the analyst and analysis" by Phyllis Greenacre. *Psychoanalytic Quarterly, 36*: 637.

Mahler, M. S. (1968). *On Human Symbiosis and the Vicissitudes of Individuation*. New York: International Universities Press.

Mayes, L. C., & Cohen, D. J. (1993). The social matrix of aggression enactments and representations of loving and hating in the first years of life. *Psychoanalytic Study of the Child, 48*: 145–169.

McDougall, J. (1980). *A Plea for a Measure of Abnormality*. New York: International Universities Press.

Midgley, N. (2012). Peter Heller's a child analysis with Anna Freud: the significance of the case for the history of child psychoanalysis. *Journal of the American Psychoanalytic Association, 60*(1): 45–69.

Minshew, N. J., Sweeney, J. A., Bauman, M., & Webb, S. J. (2005). Neurologic aspects of autism. In: F. R. Volkmar, R. Paul, A. Klin, & D. Cohen (Eds.), *Handbook of Autism and Pervasive developmental Disorder Volume 1: Diagnosis, Development, Neurobiology and Behavior* (pp. 473–514). New York: Wiley.

Mitchell, S. A. (1993). *Hope and Dread in Psychoanalysis*. New York: Basic.

Neubauer, P. B. (1987). The many meanings of play introduction. *The Psychoanalytic Study of the Child, 42*: 3–9.

Neubauer, P. B. (1993). Playing: technical implications. In: A. J. Solnit, D. J. Cohen, & P. B. Neubauer (Eds.), *The Many Meanings of Play: a Psychoanalytic Perspective* (pp. 44–53). New Haven, CT: Yale University Press.

Neubauer, P. B. (2001). Emerging issues some observations about changes in technique in child analysis. *Psychoanalytic Study of the Child, 56*: 16–26.

Novick, K. K., & Novick, J. (2005). *Working with Parents Makes Therapy Work*. New York: Aronson.

Parens, H. (1979). The development of aggression in early childhood. Northvale, NJ: Aronson.

Parens, H., Pollock, L., Stern, J., & Kramer, S. (1976). On the girl's entry into the Oedipus complex. *Journal of the American Psychoanalytic Association, 24s*: 79–107.

Person, E. S., & Klar, H. (1994). Establishing trauma: the difficulty distinguishing between memories and fantasies. *Journal of the American Psychoanalytic Association, 42*: 1055–1081.

Pine, F. (1992). Some refinements of separation-individuation concept in light of research on infants. *The Psychoanalytic Study of the Child, 47*: 103–116.

Plastow, M. G. (2015). *What is a Child? Childhood, Psychoanalysis, and Discourse*. London: Karnac.

Reich, W. (1933). *Character Analysis*. New York: Simon & Schuster.

Rhode, M., & Klauber, T. (2004). *The Many Faces of Asperger's Syndrome.* London: Karnac.

Ritvo, S. (1993). Play and illusion. In: A. J. Solnit, D. J. Cohen, & P. B. Neubauer, (Eds.), *The Many Meanings of Play: a Psychoanalytic Perspective* (pp. 234–251). New Haven, CT: Yale University Press.

Rutter, M. (2005). Genetic influences and autism. In: F. R. Volkmar, R. Paul, A. Klin, & D. Cohen (Eds.), *Handbook of Autism and Pervasive Developmental Disorders Volume 1: Diagnosis, Development, Neurobiology, and Behavior* (pp. 425–452). New York: Wiley.

Schafer, R. (1999). Disappointment and disappointedness. *International Journal of Psychoanalysis, 80*: 1093–1104.

Schmidt, E. S. (2008). Child psychoanalysis and child psychotherapy in Chicago, 1932–2008. *The Annual of Psychoanalysis, 36*: 45–6.

Schultz, R. T., Romanski, M., & Tsatsansis, K. D. (2000). Neurofunctional models of autistic disorder and Asperger's syndrome: Clues from neuroimaging. In: A. Klin, F. R. Volkmar, & S. S. Sparrow (Eds.), *Asperger Syndrome* (pp. 172–209). New York: Guilford.

Solnit, A. J. (1970). A study of object loss in infancy. *Psychoanalytic Study of the Child, 25*: 257–272.

Solnit, A. J. (2001). Introduction and historical perspective. *Psychoanalytic Study of the Child, 56*: 3–8.

Solnit, A. J., Cohen, D., & Neubauer, P. B. (Eds.) (1993). Introduction. In: *The Many Meanings of Play.* New Haven, CT: Yale University Press.

Shapiro, T. (2000). Autism and the psychoanalyst. *Psychoanalytic Inquiry, 20*: 648–659.

Shengold, L. (1999). *Soul Murder Revisited: Thoughts About Therapy, Hate, Love, and Memory.* New Haven, CT: Yale University Press.

Shuttleworth, J. (1999). The suffering of asperger children and the challenge they present to psychoanalytic thinking. *Journal of Child Psychotherapy, 25*: 239–265.

Simpson, D. (2004). Asperger's syndrome and autism: Distinct syndromes with important similarities. In: M. Rhode & T. Klauber (Eds.), *The Many Faces of Asperger's Syndrome* (pp. 25–38). New York: Karnac.

Slade, A. (1998). Representation, symbolization, and affect regulation in the concomitant treatment of a mother and child: attachment theory and child psychotherapy. *Psychoanalytic Dialogues, 8*: 797–830.

Smolen, A. G. (2009). Boys only! No mothers allowed. *International Journal of Psychoanalysis, 90*: 1–11.

Smolen, A. G. (2013). *Mothering without a Home: Attachment Representations and Behaviours of Homeless Mothers and Children.* Lanham, MD: Aronson.

Spitz, R. A. (1945). Hospitalism. *Psychoanalytic Study of the Child, 1*: 53–74.

Spitz, R. A. (1946). Anaclitic depression. *Psychoanalytic Study of the Child, 2*: 313–342.

Spitz, R. A. (1950). Relevancy of direct infant observation. *Psychoanalytic Study of the Child, 5*: 66–73.

Spitz, R. A. (1965). *The First Year of Life. A Psychoanalytic Study of Normal and Deviant Development of Object Relations.* New York: International Universities Press.

Spitz, R. A. (1983). The evolution of dialogue. In: R. Emde (Ed.), *Rene Spitz: Dialogues From Infancy, Selected Papers* (pp. 179–198). New York: International Universities Press.

Stern, D. (1985). *The Interpersonal World of the Infant.* New York: Basic.

Stern, D. (1995). *The Motherhood Constellation: a Unified View of Parent-Infant Psychotherapy.* New York: Basic.

Stern, D. N., Sander, L. W., Nahum, J., Harrison, A. M., Lyons-Ruth, K., Morgan, A. C., Bruschweilerstern, N., & Tronick, E. (1998). Non-interpretive mechanisms in psychoanalytic therapy: The "something more" than interpretation. *The International Journal of Psychoanalysis, 79*: 903–921.

Sugarman, A. (2011). Psychoanalyzing a vulcan: the importance of mental organization in treating Asperger's patients. *Psychoanalytic Inquiry, 31*: 222–239.

Thompson, C. (1954). Psychiatry. *Psychoanalytic Review, 41*: 66–92.

Topel, E. M., & Lachmann, F. M. (2008). Life begins on an ant farm for two patients with asperger's syndrome. *Psychoanalytic Psychology, 25*: 602–617.

Tronick, E. Z. (1989). Emotions and emotional communications in infants. *American Psychologist, 44*: 112–119.

Van Krevelen, F. R. (1971). Early infantile autism and autistic psychopathology. *Journal of Autism and Childhood Schizophrenia, 1*: 82–86.

Wagonfeld, S., & Emde, R. N. (1982). Anaclitic depression: a follow-up from infancy to puberty. *Psychoanalytic Study of the Child, 37*: 67–94.

Williams, M. (1987). Reconstruction of an early seduction and its after effects. *Journal of the American Psychoanalytic Association, 35*: 145–163.

Wing, L. (1991). The relationship between Asperger's syndrome and Kanner's autism. In: U. Frith (Ed.), *Autism and Asperger Syndrome* (pp. 93–121). New York: Cambridge University Press.

Winnicott, D. W. (1945). Primitive emotion and development. *International Journal of Psychoanalysis, 26*: 137–143.

Winnicott, D. W. (1950). *Aggression in Relation to Emotional Development. Collected Papers.* New York: Basic, 1975.

Winnicott, D. W. (1962). Ego integration in child development. In: *The Maturational Processes and the Facilitating Environment* (pp. 56–64). New York: International Universities Press.

Winnicott, D. W. (1969). The use of an object. *International Journal of Psychoanalysis, 50*: 711–716.

Winnicott, D. W. (1971). *Playing and Reality*. New York: Penguin Books.

Winnicott, D. W. (1978). A Reflection. In: S. Grolnick, L. Barkin, & W. Muensterberge (Eds.), *Between Reality and fantasy* (pp. 15–33). New York: Aronson.

Winnicott, D. W. (1989). Fragments concerning varieties of clinical confusion. In: C. Winnicott, R. Shepherd, & M. Davis (Eds.), *Psychoanalytic Explorations* (pp. 30–33). Cambridge, MA: Harvard University Press.

Winnicott, D. W. (1986). *Home is Where we Start From. Essays by a Psychoanalyst*. New York: Norton.

Winnicott, D. W. (1987). *Babies and their Mothers*. New York: Addison-Wesley.

Winnicott, D. W. (1996). *Thinking about Children*. Reading, MA: Addison-Wesley.

Young-Bruehl, E. (2007). Little Hans in the history of child analysis. *Psychoanalytic Study of the Child, 62*: 28–43

Zetzel, E. R. (1960). Ernest Jones: his contribution to psychoanalytic theory. *Psychoanalytic Quarterly, 29*: 127.

INDEX